PARENTS/CHILDREN/DISCIPLINE
A POSITIVE APPROACH

PARENTS/CHILDREN/DISCIPLINE
A POSITIVE APPROACH

Clifford K. Madsen, Ph.D.
Charles H. Madsen, Jr., Ph.D.
THE FLORIDA STATE UNIVERSITY

ALLYN AND BACON, INC., BOSTON

To our children—who in shaping our lives,
inevitably judge us, yet hopefully continue to love us.

CONTENTS

INTRODUCTION

An initial book for teachers entitled *Teaching/Discipline: Behavioral Principles Toward a Positive Approach* stimulated many teachers to request a modification of that book for parents. While some teachers are able to relate teaching principles to their own children in home situations, most parents often find difficulty in making these transfers.

Parents/Children/Discipline: A Positive Approach is written to help parents take advantage of the benefits from positive findings related to child rearing. It is based on principles and actual research from that group of people who call themselves "behaviorists" or behavioral psychologists.

This book is written in three parts: Part I deals with the major issues in child rearing, Part II contains over one hundred specific examples of adult/child research which should be applicable to most parent/child interactions, and Part III provides lists to help parents develop a more positive approach in dealing with children.

The most important thing to remember when reading this book is that it is not intended as a "cookbook" approach. Children are extremely different in their responsiveness to different situations. The wise use of behavioral principles will almost always lead to a positive change in behavior. However, a loose application of a quick remedy to "stop crying, lying, or bed-wetting" will probably result in failure. It is extremely important that the entire book be read carefully, studying the many ways in which behavioral principles are applied so that each parent will be able to adapt for the individual differences of each child. Even a minor problem of a child would seem to deserve that much care.

part **I**

CHILDREN AND DISCIPLINE

## chapter 1

LOVING
THE ART OF DISCIPLINE

Could it happen to us?

As Fred looked around the courtroom, he felt he was in the middle of one of those surrealistic paintings where everything is so bizarre; clocks ticked loudly, his temperature constantly changed, little objects in the room kept dripping downward, faces appeared then faded away. His wife was seated by his side, her still limp hand in his. He had looked at her a moment ago, or was it a month ago; regardless, he knew he could not look now—the pain was unbearable. Directly in front was Paul, all of them seated facing the judge. As he looked at the back of Paul's head those strange emotions started coming back—he remembered when Paul was small, the happy times scuffling around the house, Paul's big grin, the sparkle in his eyes when he was happy. Then suddenly he remembered the night the police car drove up, the police station, the detention center. He remembered the little league baseball game when Paul got hit with that bat, the days in the hospital praying he would be all right. He thought of the boy scouts—there was a fiasco, just like the trumpet he had purchased, two hundred dollars, and then after six weeks through with the band and on to something else. He thought of Paul's school work. Paul had gotten a fairly good start, he could even read a little before he went to school—then something went wrong. Why weren't the schools better anyway? What kind of things were they teaching—certainly not what he had learned and obviously not what was important for·today's kids. He remembered his own boyhood; sure he had problems but not like this. His wife's hand dropped from his lap. He glanced at the pale defeated look on her face. He looked at Paul and instantly a great well of hatred started in his stomach. How could Paul hurt his mother like this? He remembered the nights she had cried those long hours when Paul was out somewhere not giving a damn. "Probably I should have knocked off his block the first time he swore at her." But then as a father he had always tried to be understanding. It seemed that he used to be the one able to talk to Paul, but what happened? What went wrong?

The judge was speaking, "This is not the first time I've seen you, is it, son?"

Mary tried to remember that first time; oh yes, it was that little traffic ticket, not even speeding, just coasting through a stop sign and immediately juvenile court, talking to the counselor—why, she had wondered, did they make so much out of it? Fred had gotten several speeding tickets, but he paid them and that was that. Yet, there was that young counselor prying into their personal lives.

"Is this the first time, Paul?"

"No, no sir."

"The counselor's report shows that you have not been attending summer school since we last talked. Weren't you supposed to go to summer school to make up the two credits you missed last year?"

"Excuse me your honor, but you see, I took Paul with me on the road after that stealing incident. I hadn't been spending enough time with him, and I thought it would be good to take him on my eastern run."

The judge looked up at Fred, then at Mary, and then at the counselor who all the while sat observing Paul. "You were also supposed to work around the house to earn that money to pay back Sears, weren't you, Paul?" This time Mary answered, "Paul did start working, Judge, but then he came down with his asthma condition again." The judge looked down at the report and then sat back in his chair.

Mary had not slept last night; she had not slept well for a long time. She was so very worried. What was going to happen to Paul? To them all? She knew that way down deep he was a good boy, yet all this trouble and after what he said to her last night. Mary felt her insides start to drain again and began to feel that same old head pain coming on—she reached for Fred's hand. Why don't children ever realize how much we love them?

The judge kept thumbing through the big court report but finally put it down. "Paul, do you have anything to say?"

Paul looked at the judge and felt his face get hot—he was scared. Bill had told him he was really going this time, "Yeah man, right up the river, you lost it baby—lost it." Why did this have to happen to him? He looked again at the judge, then his eyes filled; he could not speak, he could only think . . . Wow! Why me? Why the hell me?

The judge started writing, the counselor shook his head as he observed Paul's self-pity—always the last stage, not guilt, no longer even anger, no pangs of responsibility or even concern for others, just hurt—deep, deep hurt as they would sit there, always feeling sorry for themselves, never for the damage they did others. Supreme irony.

"Paul, as Juvenile Judge of Lee County, I hereby commit you to the State School for Boys until you turn twenty-one or until such time as you . . ." **Could it happen to us?**

Whom do we discipline?

Many parents have drawn an artificial line between love and discipline. Some make a point for love, others discipline. The wise think they solve the problem when they say it must be both, and all are perhaps equally naive. The essential point is that we as parents must understand precisely what we mean by love and/or discipline before we begin. The major assumption of this book is that we must be concerned with how people *act* in order to evaluate behavior or to define terms. How should one know that he is loved except by the way people act toward him: what they say, how they look, how they touch; in a word, what they *do*. Attention, praise, kind words, and physical contact have been demonstrations of love for years. Who cares if someone loves you if you never receive evidence through attention, contact, or by the spoken word? While it may be possible for love to exist in total abstraction, most people are not content with such little personal involvement, especially over an extended period of time. One often hears the phrase "I'll love you no matter what." This is a good example of a meaningless cliché. Indeed very few, if any, really believe it. "No matter what" remains an abstraction that has little meaning until it is violated. That is, I'll love you until you desert me, find someone else, treat me cruelly, violate my trust, or so forth. Actually, most people do stress overt behaviors. A more fitting phrase would be, "I'll love you if you'll love me," or "I will act in certain ways with you if you will do the same."

If such statements as "I will love you no matter what" were left to idle talk, there would be little problem. When they are taken seriously, they pose a very serious problem, especially for the parent. Parents are led to believe that they should *act* as though they love children "no matter what."

One behavioral principle which we try to teach all youngsters is simple. "When you do nice things, nice things happen to you. When you do bad things, bad things happen to you." Even allowing for slight inconsistency, if we truly believed and taught in a manner conducive to this end, we would shortly have many "nice children." Yet we often violate this principle regularly by teaching a child the exact opposite. This simple principle has several perversions: (1) When you do *bad* things, nice things happen to you; (2) when you do *nice* things, bad things happen to you; (3) no matter what you do, *bad* things happen to you; and (4) no matter what you do, *nice* things happen to you (that is, I'll love you no matter what). Perhaps the saddest ramification of this last distortion is that while we treat the child, for a time, as though all behavior deserves nice consequences, we finally give up on the child at that precise point when he has finally learned exactly what we have taught him: No matter what he does, nice things happen to him! We often compound this situation with statements such as: "I've tried everything and nothing works," or "I just can't get through to that child," or "I've given him everything and this is how he repays me."

Discipline is a process whereby certain relationships (associations) are established. It is a way of behaving, which will lead to certain results. First, it must be taught; secondly, it must be learned, i.e., internalized. Love, if it is to be more than just an idea, is a way of feeling and acting conducive to productive ends. Most parents truly love their children (that is, care about them) and desire to help each child achieve his greatest potential. However, the most difficult aspect of being a loving parent is to develop the ability to sometimes withhold *overt acts* of love (ignore or disapprove) to help the child learn appropriate ways to behave. When love responses between parent and child have been previously established, we can then respond in similar kind to the child's behavior. Thus, if a child misbehaves and we actively with-hold our overt responses of love, we then teach the child that his behavior does not deserve to be followed by love responses from us. The most tragic mistakes of the parent occur when the courage to act in this way is absent, and the parent succumbs to "giving in." The child learns a perverted association: "When I do bad things, nice things happen to me." In the long run everyone suffers, but mostly the child. The authors describe this parental behavior as a "mistake of love." More appropriately it might be classified as "naiveté" or perhaps even "lack of courage." It is amazing, al-though apparent, that some people actually believe that everything a child does should be met with overt acts of love. The parent who really loves a child will have the courage to teach him proper associations. We discipline only those people we care about; others we leave alone. **Whom do we discipline?—We discipline those we love.**

Why do we discipline?

Discipline is necessary if a child is to function properly or even to be happy. We all have had the unfortunate experience of observing either children or adults who are "undisciplined." We usually refer to such people as lacking motivation, apathetic, rowdy, or even mean, spiteful, or deceitful. But why are children so classified? How do they become this way? If self-discipline is to be internalized, then how is the child to develop this attribute? The answer is obvious—*it must be learned*. Some par-ents "beg the question" by stating that it must come from *within* the child. Yet how does motivation or proper attitude get "in"? Even if some of it is already "in," will it continue to serve in the future? These are questions with which the parent must deal.

Particular behavioral patterns are learned from the external world (external stim-uli). If a child is "motivated," it is because he has learned to associate certain behav-iors with certain outcomes; that if he acts in certain ways, certain results will follow. Motivation does not exist in a vacuum; it is a way of behaving. If the parent wants a child to behave in a certain way, then the parent must structure the child's external world (i.e., control his environment) to insure that the desired behavior will be learned. The disciplined child is a child (1) who has learned to behave socially in appropriate ways, and (2) who evidences proper patterns of responses to his work. If either one of these two general categories of behaviors is absent, we usually say the child "has a problem."

We must be very careful, however, not to designate many behaviors into one or two artificial categories and believe we have solved a problem because we have arbi-trarily classified it or given it a name. People react differently to various situations (stimuli). It is very interesting to take a pencil and paper and write down one's own responses in different situations. How do we act in our homes, in church, at a football game, in business meetings, swimming, buying shoes, driving a car, getting out of an invitation, giving a speech, eating dinner, listening to beautiful music, listening to an argument? Yes, we act differently, we dress differently, we talk differently, we even smile differently in these diverse situations. If we were brave enough to list our most secret behaviors, we would probably shock those very people who believe they know us the best. It is unwise to classify behaviors into artificial categories that have to do with only a few situations. Perhaps some justification can be made for general attributes (e.g., apathetic, aggressive, boisterous, unmotivated), but such classification is extremely deceptive and at best provides only partial information.

Specificity is the key to behavioral analysis, and the parent must deal with each specific situation in order to teach proper associations. Thinking in terms of one specific behavior which occurs in a particular situation is the key to effective discipline. Because Jane is exceptionally quiet in church does not mean that she is exceptionally quiet in school. Similarly, because she does not constantly disrupt or "act up" at home does not necessarily indicate that she is "well-behaved." It is not curious that when referring to the many social skills necessary for each child we tend toward greater classification, yet with little justification considering the magnitude of individual responses to social stimuli? These classifications are even more undesirable if we consider that in our complex communication, we have developed a certain "shorthand" for descriptive purposes. Words such as "love," "motivation," and "discipline" are used as though these words had meaning apart from specific situations. It would be extremely difficult "to communicate" without using such a "short-word system." However, we should remember that each situation is different. Every particular word refers to many different behaviors, and each association merits specific consideration. We must remember to deal individually with each behavior. When speaking of discipline we must specify the nature of the situation and also the response. We must specify exactly what happens as well as when, where, and to whom. When we use the word as an abstraction referring to many separate behaviors, we must realize that definitions of discipline must be specific to certain behaviors if the teaching of proper associations is to take place. Disciplining a child, therefore, means something different in each situation if procedures are to be effective.

How then are we to get our child to learn the many behaviors that will provide him with the necessary skills to achieve a productive life? Within the complexity of his many responses to his external environment, we must structure his external world to provide proper relationships to be learned. We should not sit back and hope that motivation will somehow "get inside." Realizing the many ways a child must respond to his world, we must "set the stage" as best we can, so that he will have opportunities to learn appropriate behavior. We must structure the environment to provide the child with proper associations. Discipline must first be external: it must come from *without* before it can be from *within*.

If learned relationships to external stimuli are conducive to productive ends, the child will have a repertoire of responses that will serve him well as he meets the constant challenges of life. If he is capable of following rules, acting enthusiastically regarding new learning experiences, staying "on task" during work periods, relating well with other children and adults, knowing when to be assertive and when to acquiesce, indeed, if he has learned to respond appropriately to many specific situations, then we say he is well-disciplined. **Why do we discipline?—We discipline to provide for individual productivity and personal happiness.**

What does discipline take?

The late President Kennedy in his book *Profiles in Courage* stated the problems of the politician in facing the demands of continued popularity as opposed to acting on the courage of his convictions. Politicians are not alone in this dilemma. Many do not realize the strength of pressures placed upon parents for conformity and popularity. This pressure comes not only from children and community but also from friends and authorities. It is much easier to go along, not to rock the boat, than to reevaluate one's position, especially in relationship to "touchy problems." It *is* difficult to discipline your friend's child when he is in your home, to face the disapproval of another parent, to face an irate neighbor who insists your child has dealt with his child "unfairly," or to answer a child's touchy question honestly. It is difficult to explain a simple behavioral approach which rests on direct immediate consequences and not on intriguing deceptions. It is difficult to understand that *the question of discipline is not one of strictness or permissiveness but one of cause-and-effect relationships*. It is difficult to help your child when behavioral interactions may require opposite parent/child interactions than those you and your child are used to or patterns very different from those which have been previously established. It is difficult to live through the first day of a new program in discipline without giving in. It is most difficult to lose, for a time, the favorable response of your child.

Every person is faced with the problem of wanting to be liked. In our society being liked is an admirable goal. It is indeed easy to demand a little less, hoping to be liked. Some people's desire to be liked is so great they will suffer mild contempt for the privilege. Furthermore, while most parents do not hesitate in having their young child suffer through a medical innoculation for long term good, many haven't the courage to initiate a program of discipline which, although it might cause temporary suffering in familial interactions, would in the long run really benefit the child. In addition, children may often evaluate parents in terms of entertainment. The value of discipline is not likely to be cherished immediately. "Why didn't I have anything fun to do today?" Children may respond negatively when entertainment is not forthcoming. Nevertheless, it should be remembered that *your approval* is probably much more important to the child than *his* approval is to you. A parent's personal approval is a most effective reward. *It should not be given indiscriminately*. Indeed, one never does a person a favor by letting him get away with anything, especially that which he does not like about himself. If the parent really knows in what he believes, then he is much less likely to succumb and give in to pressures. **What does discipline take?— It takes courage.**

## chapter 2

DISCIPLINE
THE WAY TO LEARNING

What caused them to be that way?

At any time in the development of a child, we are prone to look back into the child's history to explain his present behavior. Thus, we have a never-ending spiral which assesses blame backwards and places responsiblity on something or someone in the past (behavioral antecedents). Colleges blame the public schools, public schools blame the home, and the parents often blame each other or the child's progenitors ad infinitum. If we must stop somewhere, let us stop at birth, although some theoreticians would input motives even before the child's first breath.

Let us consider three oversimplified, but rather characteristic, views of the child at birth: (1) the child is born good, (2) the child is born bad, and (3) the child is born neither good nor bad. If, as some believe, all children are born basically good, then the child's only obstacle is the corruption of living. The parent's goal would be to avoid corrupting his basic nature. This would not be difficult in a Utopian world. Perhaps it would not be difficult in the world in which we live, if all behavioral responses were predestined to be ideal. Furthermore, a problem arises when "good" is specifically defined since each person's idea of the "good" does not always coincide with another's. A second problem arises if the child has somehow been previously corrupted for now the child evidences both "good" and "bad" behavior.

The second view proposes that children are born bad. In this case the parent's job would be to correct the basic "badness" so the child could be "good." Again we have a problem with definition of "bad," especially without reference to specific overt behaviors. It is curious that many people who believe in this "badness" theory assume quite readily that children's good behavior is *not* learned but that all bad behavior (usually referring to moral transgressions) must be eliminated. Regardless, if the child has learned any "goodness" at all, he will still present a mixture of both "good" and "bad."

The third position presupposes neither good natures nor bad and, therefore, assumes that all behavior is learned. The parent's job in this situation simply would be to teach the child correct responses. Nevertheless, in all probability the child will have picked up some "bad" behaviors outside the home. Therefore, the same situation will be evidenced as with the other two positions. The important question regarding the foregoing is: What should the parent do? Regardless of philosophical orientation, or how one believes or feels about human nature, should the parent's responses to the child be any different? Indeed, *is it possible to start changing behavior at any other place than where the child is?* Susy, Sam, and Fred all lie—Susy because her sweet nature has become corrupted, Sam because he was born bad, and Fred because he learned some wrong associations. Does it really matter what their personal history or the parent's philosophy is? The important question would seem to be: What should the parent do? Even if we could solve the philosophical problem or know the particular reinforcement history of the individual children, they are still liars. All too often we pretend we have solved a problem because we can find some explanation for the behavior (e.g., high score on "problem child tests," being among bad influences, hit on the head with a bat, traumatic birth, terrible first grade teacher). Unfortunately, the children will continue to lie until something is done to change their behavior. During the very first processes of interacting with the child after a problem is specified, the parent should be able to assess the extent of the child's specific problem. These first encounters with the child usually provide all that is needed to determine where the child is. Unless the problem is medical or requires the services of a professional, the parent can begin to do something concerning the child's behavior. A long involved analysis of the child's "personality" is generally unproductive and unnecessary. **What caused them to be that way?—It does not matter.**

Who has the responsibility?

Parent *X* has a problem child. In almost every situation when he should be acting one way, he is acting another. His behavior gets constantly worse until the parent can take it no longer. The parent passes the point of feeling frustrated and, if honest, may even admit dislike toward this source of constant irritation. The parent decides to find out just what the child's problem is. After an extensive and costly battery of tests, reports, and time-consuming investigation, the parent may be given the answer: "You have a problem child." On every one of the "problem child tests" he scored extremly high. Not only did all the tests indicate that he is indeed a problem child (exhibited deviant associations), but reports concerning his life outside the home, at school, and with peers may be even worse. Parent *X* cannot help feeling pity when learning of his child's terrible adjustment and begins to wonder how he survived as well as he did. Parent *X* may discuss the situation with a close friend, and they both marvel anew at how different some children can actually be. The child continues to be a problem, but now the parents "know why" (high test scores—bad personal adjustment). The child may not even finish school: he will probably grow, continually harassing society, and perhaps end up in some of society's more stigmatized institutions. "How tragic, but what can be done with a personality like that?" Obviously nothing—the end?

Man is a complex organism. Among his many attributes is an ability for exceptional discrimination. All his empirical senses provide a basis for remarkable differentiation. At an early age (approximately six months) he can even tell the difference between people. He learns what to touch, what not to touch; he learns a complex language system; he learns auditory and visual discriminations; he learns to run and yell at playtime and to sit quietly during meals. He even learns to "put on" his parents if he can get away with it. The child's discrimination between people develops so well that he even learns which one of his parents to ask for certain privileges.

Of course the child has a "problem." That is precisely why he was sent for "testing." And how unfortunate it is that there are many "diagnosticians" whose only purpose stops after merely confirming the fear of parents—if the parents are able to understand their terminology. The child will continue to have problems until someone teaches him different responses. He has learned certain ways to deal with his world —the more he is reinforced for his deviant behavior, the more deviant will be his responses.

The truly pathetic possibility is that perhaps no one will *change his behavior*. One place where behavioral changing can begin is the home. Yet many parents abdicate responsibility for changing the child's behavior by seeking out more and more so-called explanations for why it happened. *The child can discriminate*. He can be taught new responses to deal with any part of that other world outside the home. He can learn school subjects, interpersonal skills, and new rules of social interaction to break the cycle of his past. If cooperation is impossible, he can even learn these responses *in spite of a bad neighborhood or school*.

It is not easy to deal with these children. They take time, energy, and disciplined parents. All these children do not change for the better or even survive; yet for these children *a change in behavior, not mere explanations, is their only hope*. **Who has the responsibility of discipline?—Parents.**

Why don't they learn?

Many questions have been raised recently in relationship to school work and why Johnny doesn't learn. Too often criticisms arise from sources that do not support schools with long-term tangible encouragement or positive alternatives. Instead, scathing indictments are directed toward those very individuals, teachers, and supportive parents who spend a great deal more time thinking about the question and trying to improve the situation than do most of their critics. In every aspect of learning, continued educational research is needed to assess and remediate learning difficulties. At present parents and teachers must strive together to do the best job possible.

Education is stressed in many ways in our culture. Quite naturally we often assume that everyone wants to learn. We even assume that they want to learn what we want them to learn. Some children do not want to learn. Others do not want to learn what we think they should learn. The reaction of adults when confronted with these situations should not be amazed bewilderment (any adult's reinforcement history includes values established through many years of learning) but a basic question: *Why should they want to learn?* Children must be taught to learn, that is, to establish their own goals. Also it is much easier not to learn if the entire responsibility for teaching can be given away to the schools. *Parents who do not support teachers will have children with learning problems.* A serious detriment to learning is the payoff some children receive when they can make their parents angry with school personnel. Parents who criticize, demean, argue about, and castigate schools and teachers will usually have children who do the same. This mistake concerning lack of support is very similar to the problem one parent creates when he does not present a united front with his spouse concerning the child's discipline. If parents disagree they should do so either alone or in such a manner that the child cannot play one parent off against the other or in any other way give the problem away. Such is the cooperation required between parents and teachers.

Many children *do* love to learn; yet most parents are not aware of the amount of their personal approval and other positive rewards that have gone into creating this situation.

Other children are just too comfortable to learn. Why should they learn to speak, let alone properly, if all desires are met without this particular mode of verbal symbolization? Why should one learn a difficult spelling system or an individual work task if gazing out the window passes the time better? Why should one do any school homework if one finds that more attention is received when one wanders around his room, watches TV, writes a "special note," plays with a favorite game, or does any number of more fun things than homework?

The desire to learn must be taught. Appropriate learning behaviors, such as good study habits, paying attention, or working for long periods, must be established that provide some *reward* for the child. No thinking adult wastes time in idle pursuits that are both difficult and meaningless. How can parents expect any one automatically to want to learn, especially when it may represent work? **Why don't they learn? —Because the rewards of learning have not been established.**

What if it's work?

Most people assume the responsibility of work. We speak often about work: working on a project, going to work, getting work, finishing our work, and so on. Yet in our society we have a growing tendency to turn work into play. Most parents realize the importance of making work as enjoyable as possible. When children can become excited about work they consider it play, and everyone is much happier. The ingenious parent most often strives to turn work tasks into play. Successful parents are those who are able to elicit a pleasurable response toward the most rigorous pursuits and make the most difficult task pleasant.

Unfortunately, our highly technological society has turned many work tasks into play without maintaining discipline toward those tasks that are still "work-work" tasks as opposed to "play-work" tasks. The young boy's delight in finally building his very own plane vanishes or wanes appreciably when he is presented with a common battery-propelled toy that flies instantly and can be purchased for a fraction of his allowance. Most adults will testify with pride to those endeavors which represented, for them, hard work and true discipline. Patience, repetition, and arduous industry are still required for long-term achievement and happiness in almost every activity of life. Yet we have more and more "instant avenues to success." The problem for today's parent is not only in structuring "play-work" (technology is providing wonderful aids in this regard) but also with instilling the necessary discipline for *long-term* rewards (i.e., establishing maturity). If behaviors conducive to long-term goals are not acquired early, it is much less likely they will be acquired later. If a child does not learn early in life to work hard and long for specific goals, then he is not likely to change as he grows older.

Today's society provides many entertaining activities with almost as much turnover as there are activities. The possibilities for increased involvement become greater and greater for the growing child. Almost all his time can be spent changing from one activity to another. While many parents provide veritable "toy stores" within their homes to increase choice as well as involvement, many times youngsters are still bored. Consider specialized fields such as music, art, and creative writing. How many times have we said as adults, "I'd give anything to play like that, or to paint like that, or to write like that"? Of course we would *not*. We know what it would take in time and effort. The irony is not that we do not often have such skills; it is that we do not have enough understanding concerning the importance of long-term skill acquisition to appreciate the skill evidenced in others and to insure that our children stay with an activity long enough to master it.

This observation should not indicate that the parent should take pride in being a punishing taskmaster. It is extremely unlikely that children will want to continue any activity past the formal experience of their true "reward" for learning (working) has been merely to have the gruesome experience stop. The secret for developing capacity for work is to stretch the length of time between *rewards* so that the child will strive through some misery to seek long-term goals (e.g., a college degree, writing skills, continued reading of great literature, interpersonal friendships, ongoing enjoyment in listening to music masterworks, or an insatiable desire for scientific precision).

Thus, the problem for today's parent is not only to make work tasks pleasurable, but also to develop capacity for work. *This constitutes a process of having the child work for delayed rewards over an ever-increasing time span.* **What if it's work?— Then capacity for work must be developed.**

## chapter 3

LEARNING
THE MODIFICATION OF BEHAVIOR

What is behavior modification?

Behavior is a common word which is used casually in referring to many things. The term *behavior,* as used in this book, refers to *anything* a person does, says, or thinks that can be observed directly and/or indirectly. Besides referring to specific cause-and-effect relationships, behavior modification includes techniques for changing behavior. A well-behaved child is one who behaves in ways the parent thinks are appropriate to the situation.

Principles for teaching (shaping appropriate behaviors) should not be confused with other issues. It is important that techniques of behavior modification not be confused with the use of these same techniques to implement specific values. Many parents regard the questions concerning why, what, and for whom as certainly more important than how. Therefore, after parents have decided what is to be learned and why it is to be learned (i.e., chosen their own values), a behavioral approach will help them go about teaching it. Also, we encourage parents to involve their children in these decisions whenever possible. There is a very simple rationale to explain the efficacy of behavioral approaches. Simply stated, *behavioral change must be based on a reason:* children work for things that bring pleasure, children work for approval of loved ones, children change behaviors to satisfy desires they have been taught, children avoid behaviors they associate with unpleasantness, and children act in similar ways to behaviors they have often repeated. The behavior modification approach actually comes from science and represents nothing more than simple cause-and-effect relationships.

Some might say, "Yes, but isn't that a cold approach?" Certainly not. While behavior modification is based on scientific principles verified in the laboratory, it is largely the nature of material to be learned that represents important value choices. Actually, because of its consistency and simplicity, behavioral modification applied by means of contingent reinforcement (approval-disapproval) represents a very kind and understandable system to children. The behavioral scientist who observes a home situation can behaviorally classify almost everything that goes on, regardless of how well parents understand principles of reinforcement. Cause-and-effect behaviors are always present. For example, some parents do not realize the effects of their own behavior on their children. Some do not realize when they are being sarcastic. "Why don't you just yell louder, Jimmy?" In such a situation parents unwittingly reinforce a wrong behavior and problems are created because the child is not really sure of the parent's meaning. Being taken literally is the price one pays for using sarcasm. The behavioral clinician could demonstrate how parents might be more effective in application of the parent's own values through the judicious use of behavioral principles. Many parents are actually surprised to learn how closely they approximate a fairly comprehensive behavioral approach. After being apprised of behavioral principles many exclaim, "Why, that's what I've been doing all the time!"

When learning is defined as a change or modification of behavior, then three things are necessary: (1) experience, (2) discrimination, and (3) association. For instance, a child is presented with a color (*experience*). After a time the child *discriminates* (i.e., tells the difference) between this color and other colors or the absence of this color. Through repetition, an *association*(s) is made with the color, e.g., red. The child may then evidence in some behavior, most often previously learned (e.g., pointing, matching, speaking, thinking), that he has learned the color. The preceding definition of learning based upon reinforcement theory does not quarrel with mediational processes in learning or with the material to be learned. It proposes a method to promote or expedite this learning. In short, it asks, "How should we go about teaching the color red in the best possible manner to insure correct association?" Or "How should we go about teaching the child to share, to clean his room, to obey traffic rules, and so on?" If the child responds favorably to our presentation, we assume the external stimuli (including the results which follow the behavior) are associated in a way that functions as a reward for the child; that is, we have set up the learning experience in such a way that it rewards the child. But what if the child does not respond? Then we must restructure the external environment until the child does receive proper motivation. **What is behavior modification?—It is a process for learning.**

Is behavior learned?

The impetus for behavioral theory, or reinforcement theory, or whatever one chooses to call behavioral principles, substantially grew from the works of B. F. Skinner. "Programmed instruction" is the best-known result of this initial work, as are many other "systems" relating to teaching, treating mental illness, behavioral research, and clinical psychology. Indeed, the entire rationale concerning behavior modification is that behavior is *learned. All behavior.* Behavior thusly defined includes emotional responses, attitudes, reading, listening, talking, looking into the mirror, liking a person, wanting to talk out a problem, hitting, being frustrated, staying "on task," getting "off task," responding appropriately to the desires of a parent, acting contrary to the desires of parents, all "good" behavior, all "bad" behavior, disturbing the home, being well-behaved, being excited about school work, hating to learn, and so on—and so on—and so on.

The most basic reductions of reinforcement theory as an explanation to assess a person's responses at any given time are: (1) a person has *not learned,* (2) he has learned *correct associations* (appropriate behavior), or (3) he has learned *incorrect associations* (inappropriate behavior). Exactly the same principles are used to teach good social behavior as are used to teach appropriate work skills. If the parent wishes that children have a real desire to learn something, the parent must structure the external environment by providing approval contingencies so children will seek these previously established rewards for appropriate behavior. After initial manipulation the rewards for proper behavior will often come from the reinforcement of the particular task itself. Incidentally, this is precisely what most parents do when they initially make a "game out of working." The children become enthused concerning the game per se, not realizing it is a subtle hoax to stimulate effective work. Curiously, some parents who try desperately to make working "fun" also say they reject any "manipulation techniques." The parent's job is to structure the child's experiences. This structuring process involves manipulating the environment (i.e., setting up the correct situation) conducive to effective learning; whether the goal be simple obedience, complex problem solving, or spiritual values. It would seem that parents should structure as wisely as possible. One should know the subparts necessary to any complex task (e.g., cleaning one's room, being alone, entertaining oneself, reading, completing a hobby project) and structure the situation in order that each child has a "rewarding experience." It can be seen that even in many of our most cherished clichés, we allude to behavioral manipulation. It appears paradoxical for the parent to reject manipulation when this is indeed the essence of what the parent is already doing.

Behavioral research demonstrates that if tasks can be: (1) geared to the child at his own level, (2) presented in logical sequences, with (3) the child being told when he is making correct/incorrect responses, and (4) contingent rewards given for coming closer and closer (successive approximations) toward defined goals, then the child will certainly learn. Exactly the same principles apply to teaching appropriate behavior as apply to teaching proper social skills. **Is behavior learned?—Yes.**

Who decides who decides?

Power, by whatever name, is one of the most contingent of all behavioral interactions. When referring to physical objects in motion such as the power of a moving automobile to damage a person's body, few people question the power of the car; they question only the intent, skill, or responsibility of the driver. Some people seem to assume power over other people; others manifest power which is thought to be given to them, for example, the power of elected officials to enforce laws. Literary sources often portray individuals seeking power—others avoiding it. Most of us, however, choose to either relabel "power" (especially in this age of the euphemism) or to pretend that power actually does not exist. We prefer, instead, to talk about responsibility, duty, or rights, as in the essay "Who has the responsibility?" in Chapter 2. Perhaps most of us would like to believe that nobody has power over us and anything we might say or do would be only by choice. Often it frightens us to realize the power that does exist—especially the power we have over our children. Not only are adults usually bigger (at least for a little while), but most of us think faster than children and, therefore, are able to "snow" them. We fix the television with just a small adjustment or replace a tube, cartoons reappear, and the children look at us as though we are electronic wizards. We repair their bicycles or the lawn mower, we sew a favorite dress or put some magic balm on a cut or bruises, or read to them, or answer a difficult question—*the awe and respect of little children is very reinforcing to adults.*

Often we use our sophistication to manipulate them into doing something which they do not think about, "Would you like to put your pajamas on in the bedroom or the front room?" We do not ask them, "Do you choose to go to bed?" It seems that most often we do about "everything in our power" in order to impose our value system on them. "Wash your hands and brush your teeth before . . . take off those dirty things before you come in here . . . now we do want your room to be clean, don't we . . . of course you don't take money from mother's purse without asking . . . etc." It would appear that most of what we just assume to be the correct thing to do represents the imposition of our value system upon the child. Probably most of the "acculturating process" or teaching of "good" behavior actually represents the imposition of values, whether these values come from home, school, community, church, or elsewhere. Who decides a child should read, write, spell, not steal, or finish school? Adults who have not thought about these activities in regard to "imposing their values" sometimes become extremely upset and state, "Well, how do you expect the child to live a happy life or get a decent job or anything else! I can't sit by and watch my child burn himslf or run out into the street. Do you expect me to be silent when I know she's ruining her life with that boy?" At the same time parents may say, "I do want my children to think for themselves, and I want them to establish their own values. . . ."

Parents who do not make clear differentiations in their own thinking about who decides who decides, will probably have many problems. Parents are charged legally with imposition of certain values concerning their children's behavior. Many would say that ethically parents ought to be responsible for most of the child's behavior, and some would say that this is precisely what being a parent is all about: to instill within each child the selected best from the parents' experience in order that the child will be able to function productively. Regardless, *who decides* is not nearly as difficult a question as *who decides who decides,* for most parents truly want their children to be able to make decisions for themselves. Therefore, parents decide to allow their child to make relatively unimportant decisions: When do you choose to clean your room? Where can you be reached in case of emergency? Which job do you choose to do? Who is it you will be going with? Where do you want to go to college? Parents who start early to teach their children both to understand the nature of power and how to use it, might insure that children will be better able to deal with apparent inequities as children mature. Some parents refer to this structuring, in which precise definitions and specific responsibilities are firmly established, as "defining limits" and/or specifying acceptable behavior. Examples of this structuring might include interpersonal and sibling relationships, propriety, honesty, and so on. If a child is taught early that a parent is not an electronic wizard, master fixer, or all-knowing genius; that parents do not always evidence perfect taste, heal all wounds, or even "understand" some of the later ones, then the child might not have to be so disenchanted when he inevitably discovers parents' limitations. If a parent states precisely what power resides with the parent and what decisions rest with the child, perhaps the child will strive continuously to earn more privileges rather than feel sorry for himself because he is not permitted a certain activity. Issues regarding power are not easy to think through nor are their behavioral contingencies or antecedents easy to establish. Problems relating to power are much like issues concerning "fairness," in that they are based upon the values of all individuals concerned. Some parents, even after many years, have not established who decides who decides regarding major issues concerning themselves and their spouses. It should not be surprising, then, if familial problems occur, especially as children grow older, for as the years pass parents and children must often decide to *agree to disagree* if any harmony is to prevail. Anger is not reinforced in relationship to those decisions that a child definitely believes are not his. Anger is reinforced only with those decisions which he believes ought to be within his own control and not someone else's. **Who decides who decides?—As far as the child is concerned, parents.**

Who has the problem?

Perhaps one of the most challenging tasks for today's parents is to know what literature to believe and what to reject, which authority to respect and which to discount. In our multimedia world we seem to have experts by the score with almost as many kinds of advice as we have experts. Presumably many parents are saying, "Why don't they get together; one says that what is right today was wrong five years ago; what we got when we were growing up was wrong or another says it was right, depending upon which one you read." The authors are very sympathetic to this situation especially since we are constantly dealing with parents' and children's problems, including our own. It is our strong belief, however, that many problems may be actually "caused" by reading and acting upon some of the pronouncements found in many articles. Parents come to us constantly with "children's problems" that did not exist before an article was read. We are reminded of the man who worried for twenty years about latent fear, until the day he decided he didn't have to worry about it as long as it was latent.

It would be less than honest for the authors to presume that we also are not advising; we certainly are, and it should be stated that *severe problems should be taken to a professional.* However, it is our hope that parents will rely on their own honest assessments concerning most child rearing. It appears to us that *honesty* is a major key to behavioral assessment by parents, even if parents are being advised by professionals. If one is honest, one will not *give his problem away and absolve responsibility*. The attribute of giving a problem away is perhaps best illustrated by a story concerning a graduate student in psychology who was presenting to a graduate seminar the case of his first interview with a client. He was apologizing to the other members of the seminar, "I guess I fouled up. About the only thing that I established was that the client had a studying problem." One of the older supervisory clinicians rose to his feet, smiled at the young man, picked a little at his pipe and addressed the group, "As some of you know, I was an obstetrician before I changed to this type of clinical work, and I didn't learn much from my previous medical speciality that had immediate transfer. I did learn one thing, however, and that concerns *who's pregnant!* You know, the very first time a patient came to me, the one thing I tried to firmly establish was who's pregnant. 'No, *we're* not going to have a baby, your *husband's* not going to have a baby, your *mother's* not going to have a baby, your *family's* not going to have a baby—you, *you're* the one who is going to have a baby.' It was always amusing to me to see some of the expectant mothers trying to give their problem away. Of course, it was they who had to eat properly, receive proper medical attention when needed, go through the entire pregnancy, and so on." He continued, "Son, if within that first session with your client you established *who* had the problem, you succeeded. If your client left realizing that her studying difficulty was not her roommate's problem or her professor's problem or her mother's problem or her counselor's problem, then you are well on your way."

Assessing who has the problem requires a parent to decide if the problem really belongs to the child or to the parent. Often both have a problem: the child, an inappropriate behavior which needs to be changed—the parent, the responsibility to do something about changing it. Many times, however, the problem is not real. Sometimes the only real problem is in the heads of the parents. After reading some article, the parents begin to worry about a potential problem, sometimes to the extent that they change their interaction patterns with the child and actually create the very problem they suspect. Certainly, these "self-fulfilling prophesies" should be avoided, especially when the suspected problem cannot be identified as overt behavior(s) but refers only to an idea such as inferiority, lack of love, need for self-expression, need for individual achievement, or other nonspecified concepts.

While parents are advised to be self-reliant in behavioral assessment of children's problems, parents should also be careful not to believe that inappropriate behavior is *just a stage* the child is going through. If by "stage" we mean precisely the length of time that a child exhibits incorrect responses until something is done to insure improved behavior or if by "stage" we mean those behaviors quite proper for one age but not for another, then there is no cause for concern—still no reason for alarm. If, however, we refer to "stage" in an attempt to *give away our problem,* hoping that in some mysterious manner a day will come when the problem magically goes away, then perhaps we should reevaluate. The very young child's occasional "disrobing" should not be equated with his occasional "lie." Social situations within the child's world will probably change his clothes wearing behavior but probably not his lying. The child who occasionally "forgets to clean his room" should not be equated with the child who occasionally "has severe temper tantrums." The child who occasionally "refuses to share his toy" is not comparable to a child who "plots to put himself up by secretly bringing physical harm or reprimand by making a younger sibling cry." Classifying problems into "normal stages of development" should be done with great care.

Parents should realize that even seemingly unimportant behaviors probably change because something or someone in the child's environment acts in modifying the child's responses—that is, some problem behaviors will be decreased or eliminated when the older child's interaction with his environment promotes different expectations; but, other problems will *intensify*. The extent to which these problem behaviors change is determined by the cause-and-effect relationships interacting within the child's world, not by magic or by just growing older. There are many old liars, parents who constantly loose their temper, and adults who scheme in putting down other colleagues, workers, or even friends to get ahead. Being honest, there are adults who are exhibitionists, extremely messy, and even stingy. **Who has the problem?—You decide.**

## chapter 4

BEHAVIOR
THE CONTINGENT RESULT OF LIFE

The reader has been exposed to some basic questions regarding discipline. This chapter offers instruction in analyzing *how to discipline*. Some principles presented are designed to deal with inappropriate behavior, although it should be kept in mind that all principles apply equally as well to appropriate responses (i.e., wholesome learning).

What is the payoff?

A traditional viewpoint regarding child rearing prevalent in today's society is to focus upon many past events (reinforcement history) leading toward a particular behavioral goal, rather than upon the manipulation and control of the present environment. As has been previously stated, this procedure of looking backward in time is both unproductive and unnecessary, especially when it is used as an excuse for not taking the responsibility to solve current problems. When the parent desires to change a child's specific inappropriate behavior, the parent should first attempt to *find the payoff* and eliminate it if at all possible. *Behavior that goes unrewarded will extinguish* (decrease). The parent must observe the child carefully to determine the payoff. The parent must also recognize individual differences; the payoff is often different for each child. For example, at home children *A, B,* and *C* fight over activities and games. After many warnings their father finally intervenes and sits them down for a long talk on cooperation. This is just exactly what child *A* wanted. Dad never spent time with her when there was not a family crisis, but now she had finally managed to goad him into "punishing" her. Child *B* just liked to make his sister angry. Every time she got mad it just "broke him up." He knew he was bothering her, and he enjoyed her distress—Wow! She gave him such *stern* looks and complained so much. During the talks with Dad she even cried a lot. Child *C* is not old enough to care about the communication sessions, but he does like to play with his older brother and sister. Every time the older people talk, however, Dad gives him a special treat so he will not feel "left out." When children *A, B,* and *C* finish their "cooperation" session Dad will probably feel much better. Tomorrow the children will continue to fight—even more.

Parents who have simple one-sided explanations for all inappropriate behavior will generally be ineffective. "All those children need is a little love." "The thing they need is a good hard paddling." "Get them out in the world; then you'll see how they do." "They need a decent place to play and express themselves." "They need a professional who truly understands their problem." The difficulty with this type of analysis is that it is not differentiated or individualized. There are some children who may fit one, none, or all the above categories plus countless others. The one thing that children exhibiting inappropriate responses *do* need is a person who can find the payoff. What is maintaining the problem, keeping the behavior alive? Behavior is a result of its consequences. If the payoff for the child can be found and completely eliminated, then the behavior will gradually extinguish—*if consistency is maintained.*

A word of caution is important, however. One important result of eliminating the payoff is that the undesired behavior will first get worse before it gets better. The parent must remember that the child has learned to behave in ways to get what he wants. When the "reward" is eliminated, most children will try harder (i.e., the inappropriate behavior increases) before coming to realize that there is no payoff. After the initial surge the behavior will extinguish. Many people give up during the storm before the calm. "Oh, I've tried ignoring, but the baby cried even louder." Of course.

Finding the payoff can be difficult, and sometimes the payoff comes from a source that the parent cannot control. For example, the child's peers, physiological reactions, the school, the other parent, internal imagery, and so on. Nevertheless, many problems can be solved by eliminating the reward. **What is the payoff?—That which keeps the behavior alive.**

The above parent might provide child *A* with a pleasant talk when nothing is wrong or preferably after cooperative play with the youngest child *C*. The parent might separate child *B* from his sister and/or teach her how not to reinforce her brother's problems.

What constitutes reward?

After a parent determines the payoff for a particular behavior and eliminates it, the parent will soon observe a decrease in undesirable behavior. Sometimes this alone is all that is needed. Yet more often other things in the child's environment (stimuli) must be controlled; that is, other contingencies must be structured in order to discipline. It is better to start with just one behavior and not try to eliminate everything simultaneously, unless the parent has a great deal of help and can initially devote all available time just to behavioral problems. If many undesired behaviors are prevalent, parents are advised to establish a priority and start with the inappropriate behavior that most interferes with proper responses. It is extremely important that parents deal with *overt behaviors,* not ideas (for example, "getting to school on time" as opposed to "a bad attitude about school"). It is also advisable to make up a set of easily understood rules for each activity. In making up the contingencies (i.e., structuring the rewards) the new payoff for desirable behavior (following the rules) must be known, tangible, and close enough to the child's own behavioral responses to motivate him to seek it. Initially it is far better to give too much reward than not enough. The idea is to get the child "winning" as soon as possible. For general control in the early years words, contact, and expressions are highly effective; group activities and peer group approval provide powerful rewards for the adolescent years; money and individual activities for young adults. Various "token systems" are generally effective at all age levels and come closest to representing our own monetary system. For young children correct responses can earn "tokens" that are exchanged for tangible goods (e.g., most young children enjoy things such as toys, trips, playthings, or food). Tokens may be chips, papers, check marks, or anything convenient. Rewards earned for tokens should have specified values (i.e., candy bar = five points, trip to ice cream store = eight points, commercial game = ten points, glider plane = fifteen points) so that children can receive tangible credit for exhibiting appropriate behaviors, such as following specific rules. Each child can have a small notebook, kept by either parents, children or both, and at appropriate intervals (after play time, before supper, following clean-up, etc.) the parent marks the child's points. The parent may begin a program by displaying rewards and asking the child which one he is working toward. Then the parent may go over the rules. The young child's rules should be written down in a conspicuous place and explained daily—at a time other than when they have been violated: We sit quietly during meals and ask properly for food. We say "excuse me" before we interrupt to talk. We stay in our own room during study time unless given permission to leave. We play gently with little sister and do not hit, etc. At opportune times the parent writes down the points. The very act of recording may be used as an effective control. It is critical for the parent to try very hard to *catch the child being good* and reward him with points paired with words and expressions of praise instantaneously. In addition, all or part of a child's allowance can be used as a contingent reward.

In the initial stages of control it is important to have the child achieve success quickly, after which the time between behavior and reward may be stretched for longer periods while continuing to pair appropriate personal responses from the parent (words of praise, expressions such as smiling, and closeness such as positive touching). In time the personal approval of the parent, and later, the child's approval of himself will probably be all that is needed for proper motivation. This is certainly what most parents desire, but in order to achieve this level of sophistication, one must start where the child is. Some children seem to be amenable to smiling, pleasing parents, or being obedient. Others have to learn appropriate responses through more tangible rewards. Token systems may be set up at all levels of sophistication in preparation for adult employment.

One extremely effective technique for small children is the use of food (candy, juice, flavored cereal) as contingent reinforcement. The parent may start the very first day of the new program with a "goodie" party. The parent gives the child a treat and while the child is eating the parent says, "We will have another "goodie" party if you are quiet while I count to ten." (The parent then counts aloud quickly, making sure the child wins.) After giving the candy the parent says, "If you are quiet for five minutes we will have another party, but if you talk we will not have one." Now the parent sits back and waits; in all probability the child will talk, whereupon the parent says, "Oh, I'm *very sorry*. You talked before our time was up; now we will not have a party. Maybe tomorrow we may have one if you are quiet." (Some children may get angry and claim this is not "fair.") *Because the parent does not get angry at the child, the child cannot give his problem to the parent.* Thus, the child receives no approval or disapproval from the parent so there is no "payoff." Instead of interacting directly with the child it may be better to use vicarious reinforcement and modeling using other brothers and sisters. To use this technique the parent chooses the child who behaves the best for this particular task and says, "I surely like the way Sheila is sitting so quietly. If all of you were acting like Sheila, we could have our party." Sometimes the parent may wish to give rewards to those children who were quiet and not give anything to those who were not. (Sheila may not think this is fair.)

The use of family or play group approval-disapproval is very effective, particularly with older children. When activities are given or denied, contingent upon the behavior of all concerned, the children themselves will take the responsibility for discipline, and discipline will start to evolve from within the familial or neighborhood group. *Peer approval* is extremely important to teen-agers. This is precisely the reason for such high esprit de corps in many group organizations, such as band, athletics, social clubs, gangs, and so on. When parents as well as the other children are taught to cut out the payoff for a particular individual's inappropriate behavior, the child's undesired behavior will generally decrease. Sometimes parents choose to verbally disapprove of certain behaviors. Of course, children may indeed be embarrassed after receiving such responses from their parents or especially from their peers—so be it. It is precisely this contingent embarrassment that solves the problem. If children do not care what others think of them, then withholding of approval or verbal disapproval is not effective. It is the parents' value system that determines what contingencies are to be used. Contingencies, in both approving and disapproving ways, which the parent *can* use include: (1) words (spoken and written—rules), (2) expressions (facial—bodily), (3) closeness (nearness—touching), (4) activities and privileges (social—individual), and (5) things (tokens, materials, food, playthings, money). Other than the rewards of the activity itself (sometimes there are none), these categories constitute the *entire resources* the parent has for structuring. Parents should develop them well. (Study the examples and lists in Parts II and III.) **What constitutes reward?—That which the child will work toward.**

Is the world fair?

For years parents have been describing the uniqueness of their children. "All children are not alike," they say. "Each child has many different experiences," "children have different temperaments," or "they need individual attention." One would assume from this dedication to individual difference that parents would interact differentially and meet the discipline problems of each child in a unique manner, but this does not seem to be the case. Most parents also seem preoccupied with an *undifferentiated* concept of "fairness."

Children do not have a problem with undifferentiated "fairness" until someone teaches it to them. Usually it is taught by their parents. With little hesitation, parents will talk at length about how different their children are. Equally without hesitation, they try as hard as possible to be "fair." Fred and Jane are different in many, many ways. They like different things, they respond differently, and one child is almost always older. Yet, when Fred goes, Jane goes; when Jane gets candy, Fred must have candy. If Fred receives a toy, Jane must also. Fred and Jane learn quickly: "Why can't I stay up late?" "Why don't I get to go?" "How come I don't get a present?" "Why does she always get the biggest apple?" Thus Mother and Dad spend a great deal of time and energy trying to be "fair." They also create much anxiety for themselves by not admitting that they do treat the children differently and from time to time may actually even like one child more than another. These are all unnecessary attempts designed to solve the problem of undifferentiated fairness they have created for themselves. "But Fred, your birthday will come next month." "Jane, you see Fred is older than you; that's why he stays up later." "Ok, if you're going to fight over who gets the bigger apple, neither one of you can have one."

People *are* different. Some are extremely different, particularly if they have physical or mental handicaps. It would seem that the kindest interaction with children would be to instruct them in this regard—let them know that the world is not always "fair." Prepare them for the suffering they will endure because of others' mistakes. Let them realize from the beginning that their efforts are not always evaluated fairly. Help them understand that in a democracy or a family the group often suffers from the actions of a few. Let them realize that occasionally they will be punished for things that they do not do. Teach them to understand that justice is an ideal, less often a reality. *Yes, and also instruct them to be just in their own personal behaviors but not always to expect it from others.* Some of the gravest problems encountered by children come from an undifferentiated concept of "fairness."

Fairness is not a simple matter. Men have labored for centuries to ascertain "what's fair" in relationship to many different situations (laws). In the larger social context most adults deal continuously with differential assessments. Jobs are assigned differentially, as are salaries, advancement in one's profession, opportunities to achieve, and so on. How naive then to equip the child with one social response (fairness) the parent knows will cause him problems as he matures. The parent also loses a most effective technique (family approval-disapproval) when refusing to use others in the family in "shaping up" individuals, for to punish one child because of the actions of another does not seem "fair." Ideally, proper interaction patterns will eventually evolve from within each subgroup. Children will help discipline each other, not by punishing or "tattling" but by ignoring, attending to what is proper, not talking or listening to each other when they should not be, and generally *staying on task;* however, discipline will not evolve from the family unless parents use the family to bring particular actions of individuals "in line." (Some parents mistakenly believe that children should act as if they love all siblings "no matter what.")

No one wishes to be punished for another's actions. However, in cooperative societies this goes on continuously. If elected officials in a representative government decide to enter a war, they do not ask the individual child. If that child in the bud of maturity is drafted, fights, and subsequently dies in battle, then who suffers? Why not prepare children for the world in which they live where everyone's life is affected by the acts of others? Let them realize early that if within the family as well as within the larger society we are to function, we must take the responsibility and the results of interacting with others—we do not stand alone. It would seem wise to help each child understand that "what's fair" is a very big question relating differentially to almost all aspects of life. Do not prepare them for certain disillusionment with one undifferentiated response. Help them discriminate between the many issues of fairness and be prepared to deal realistically with these discernments. Children may come then to accept life's inequities while doing something to change many of them, rather than just feeling sorry for themselves because they find some aspects of interaction "unfair." When parents deal with fairness, optimism need not suffer— only naiveté. **Is the world fair?—Sometimes.**

Con contingencies be structured?

The basic premise of using reinforcement interaction effectively is to arrange the external world to shape the behavior of the child—to structure the environment so that the child receives approval-disapproval reinforcements contingent upon appropriate/inappropriate behavior. Therefore, *reinforcement interaction is the structure of approval and disapproval reinforcers across time in precise intervals to shape desired behavior toward specific goals.* A large body of research with children demonstrates that: (a) if a child knows specifically what is expected of him, and (b) he wants to do it, then (c) he probably will. The necessity for specific measurable goals (expectations) for children has already been mentioned. The crux of the problem rests with (b): arranging the contingencies of reinforcement so that the child will want to do what the parent expects.

Five techniques used in structuring contingencies are:

1. Approval (rewards)
2. Withholding of approval (withholding rewards—hope)
3. Disapproval (punishment)
4. Threat of disapproval (fear)
5. Ignoring (not attending in any manner)

Approval is easily understood. Approval is anything that is generally thought to be related with "happiness": *Words* used as praise; *expressions,* such as smiling; *closeness,* such as embracing or touching; *activities* with loved ones; *things,* such as money, clothes, cars, etc. Parents must be sure, however, that what they believe is functioning as positive reinforcement is truly positive (some children don't like ice cream).

Withholding of approval (withholding rewards) is used when the positive reinforcer functions to produce hope for the attainment of a reward the next time when the behavior is improved. In a way this procedure functions as "punishment" (disapproval), although with potentially greater effect for improvement and less wear and tear on everyone concerned. Parents may also place the responsibility for improvement upon the child and perhaps avoid negative emotional reactions directed toward themselves following punishment. "I'm sorry you didn't finish on time. Now you cannot go out to play. Perhaps tomorrow you will finish on time. Then you may play."

Disapproval is also easily understood. Disapproval is generally synonymous with what most persons term *unhappiness.* Disapproval comes in such forms as *words* when one is getting yelled at; *expressions,* such as frowning; *closeness* when one is being hit or placed in isolation; *activities,* as when we are deprived of something we want or made to do an unpleasant task; and *things,* such as feared objects. The parent must also be careful not to conclude too easily what constitutes disapproval. Children may often exhibit many inappropriate, maladaptive, and perverted associations. "I like to get spanked." "I enjoy making my mother angry." Extreme disapproval (corporal punishment) should be used very sparingly, if at all. Perhaps the most important thing to be remembered about physical punishment is that if parents decide to use it, *it should be strong enough to stop the behavior immediately and eliminate the problem at once,* otherwise parents may only insure that the child will engage in similar behavior in the future and, therefore, punishment will probably intensify, especially if parents become angry and do not realize that they themselves are contributing to the problem. Many children have been gradually conditioned to endure severe beatings, usually *without* a decrease in maladaptive responses.

Threat of disapproval (fear) should be used rarely, yet it is profoundly effective once the knowledge of disapproval is established. Individuals learn how to behave in order to avoid disapproval (unpleasant consequences): "I am careful when crossing the road to avoid getting killed"; "I don't play with guns because I could get shot"; "I study so I won't fail"; "I act appropriately in church so as to avoid the disapproval of my father." While fear is an extremely effective suppressant of much inappropriate behavior it does little to establish the joy of learning and living. Children (or adults) who are completely negatively motivated are usually tense, unenthusiastic, quiet, shy, passive, and generally fearful. Some of these children do eventually succeed, although this negatively motivated "success" usually comes at the high price of guilt, compulsiveness, generalized anxiety, and perhaps later, even ulcers.

Ignore—just that—ignore.

The formula in Figure 1 represents interaction for behavioral shaping.

			PARENT BEHAVIOR			
C **B** **H** **E** **I** **H** **L** **A** **D** **V** **I** **O** **R**		*Approval*	*Withholding of Approval*	*Disapproval*	*Threat of Disapproval*	*Ignore*
	Appropriate	Yes	No	No	No	No
	Inappropriate	No	Yes	Yes*	Yes	Yes**

* Unless payoff.   ** Unless dangerous.

Figure 1

The parent is advised, if at all possible, to use primarily approval, withholding of approval, and ignoring in controlling behavior. There is some indication that these "positive approaches" may be more effective, but, more important, *much less damage can be done than through the use of extreme disapproval (punishment)*. This does *not* mean the parent should be permissive. It indicates that as parents structure the child's environment contingent on appropriate behaviors (that is, produce appropriate cause-and-effect relationships), they should diligently try to do so through the use of "positive" techniques and structuring incompatible responses. Withholding an overt love response seems much more kind than corporal punishment. Alternately, there are times when disapproval (punishment) might need to be used. Some maladaptive behaviors of children are much worse than the punishment it could take to eliminate them. **Can contingencies be structured?—They must!**

## chapter 5

LIFE
THE STRUCTURE OF ACTIVITIES IN TIME

Is time important?

Thank you, reader. Thank you for what? Thank you for reading the next paragraph. You have not read it yet? Oh.

Why is the preceding paragraph rather absurd? It is because the "thank you" comes before the fact. Therefore, it has little meaning and even less significance in modifying your behavior (except perhaps in creating confusion). In all research concerned with behavior, no one has ever been able to teach anything through the use of antecedent rewards (rewards given before the work is done). *Rewards must come after the fact.* Thus, we enter the most elusive aspect of behavioral shaping— time. All events take place in some time interval. B. Franklin had this maxim: "Dost thou love life? Then do not squander time, for that is the stuff life is made of."

One of the most basic differentiations of the growing child comes in his progressive sophistication regarding time. Even adults cannot really tell time, as evidenced by the watches we strap to our arms. Man's temporal span is exceedingly short, and our assessment of ongoing time becomes humorous (try to estimate a minute without counting to yourself). Even with a minute you must "fill it up with something" in order to approximate the passage of time. Now consider these foolish temporal contingencies: One year old: "Baby knows I'll pick her up after I finish my work." Three year old: "Tomorrow we will go out to play." Six year old: "Be good, next week is party time." Nine year old: "When you get to be eleven you may join the scouts." Thirteen year old: "If you pass all your classes you may have a car when you're sixteen." Sixteen year old: "You must graduate from high school if you expect to have a good life." College freshman: "Study diligently, and you will be a success." If these sequences sound long, try a few out on yourself just to see how close a contingent reward or punishment must be in time to motivate you. "One more drink and tomorrow morning, wow!" "Better stop this late discussion—8:00 A.M. comes early," or "You don't have the money—why not just charge it?" As you can see, your temporal motivation is *not* long at all. Of course you realize the necessity of working toward or avoiding all those things, but they are up there in time somewhere—not now—not close enough in time to really motivate *you*.

If contingent rewards/punishments for behavior are to be effective, they must take place immediately, and *the parent must always know, before the fact, just what the contingencies are to be*. With small children this is tremendously important. "Daddy's going to spank you when he gets home" is a typical example of a ridiculous contingency.

It is also important to correct any deviant behavior before it becomes full-blown—to nip it in the bud. The parent who believes that a small disturbance "will get better" is right. It will get better and better and *better!* Full-blown disorder is usually encouraged by hesitation and caused by self-deception. *Initial stages of control are the most important*. As the child matures, his temporal span will increase *if* he is taught proper behaviors while progressively lengthening the time between action and consequence. If the bag of oats is too close to the horse, he eats the oats; if the bag is too far away, he does not move. *Time and the control of reinforcement schedules across time is imperative*. Reinforcements can be delivered on different schedules relating to time intervals or tasks completed and can be fixed or variable. The job of the parent is to start with the child where he is and then progressively take him to the point where he will be content to wait for longer and longer rewards while still exhibiting proper behavior (e.g., structuring progressive work tasks toward school grades or monthly allowance). Actually, many people guard time more jealously than anything over which they have control. *The art of living evolves from the structure of meaningful activities in time*. **Is time important?—Time is life.**

Is consistency difficult?

If one were to take the principle, "Behavior that is partially reinforced is the most difficult to extinguish," and devise a system whereby he could make a million dollars through its use, one might come up with gambling. Gambling is an activity that represents partial reinforcement at its best. If a gambler knows he will always lose, he will not gamble. Obviously he cannot always win, so the trick is to structure the environment (e.g., set the odds in a machine or roulette wheel) so that he *wins* often enough to *lose* his money in the long run).

Such is the case with other behavior. The child does not remember the 1,231 times he went to bed at 8:00 P.M. He remembers the two times he stayed up. The nine year old does not really believe that his mother will send him to "the time-out room (isolation) for ten minutes." This is already the sixth time she has threatened and nothing has happened yet. The fourteen year old stole before and didn't get caught; why should he get caught this time? The parent has paid bills late before; why should this outfit get so excited?

Inconsistency teaches just that—inconsistency. At best it produces gambling children, at worst large scale mental illness. *The most difficult task for the parent is consistency!* Parents should plan how contingencies are to be structured, make the rules, and *follow through*. The only thing that you teach a child when you break the rules is just that—to break the rules. How pathetic it is to observe children who have many severe maladaptive behaviors that have been paid off and therefore allowed to fester for longer and longer periods because of partial reinforcement. It is much like *favorable* responses; we stretch the temporal spans between reinforcements to provide longer periods of *productive* activity. Concerning maladaptive responses some children's reinforcement history contains so much partial reinforcement they will fight for weeks and months before giving up their learned behaviors. Often, it is these children who need the help of a professional. **Is consistency difficult?—It is the most difficult aspect of discipline.**

If at first you don't succeed?

If behaviors can be learned, they can also be unlearned or relearned. Sometimes, in our zeal to get through to our children, we make mistakes. Sometimes regardless of zeal, we make mistakes. The effectiveness of behavioral techniques with *severe* problem behaviors within mental hospitals and institutions for the retarded and handicapped should give us the courage to move forward. Behavioral techniques have demonstrated that even severely handicapped children can learn much faster and a great deal more than we previously believed possible.

Since it is impossible for the child to maintain two contradictory responses at precisely the same time, the skillful parent will structure to elicit responses *incompatible* with deviant behavior. "Count to ten before you get angry; think before you begin your work; take three big breaths before you cry; speak softly so we can have a 'soft' argument; now we are practicing *good* manners; let's take a break so we can begin with freshness; I'll close the curtain so the outside will not distract us; let's put our other toys away before we begin the new activity," and so on. Severe disapproval (punishment) alone may stop inappropriate behavior, but it will not necessarily teach a correct association. The child who is hit with his spoon because he cannot use it properly will not necessarily learn proper etiquette. Similarly, the child who is punished for his faulty reading will not necessarily learn to read efficiently. The one child might shun the spoon; the other child may stop reading. Setting up incompatible responses is perhaps the most effective behavioral technique because it constitutes a double-edged approach. Not only is the inappropriate behavior eliminated, but a correct response replaces it. Thus the child unlearns and relearns at the same time. It should be obvious that in this case the child's appropriate responses are directly proportional to decreases in inappropriate responses. That is, as bad behavior goes away appropriate responses replace what used to be incorrect responses. This procedure eliminates the need for much disapproval (punishment) and at the same time teaches correct associations. However, parents must deal with *overt* behaviors. *It is much easier to act your way into a new way of thinking than to think your way into a new way of acting.*

Four principles * for the parent are:

* These principles were adapted from the work of O. R. Lindsley, "Teaching Teachers to Teach," a paper presented at the American Psychological Association Convention, New York, September, 1966.

1. *Pinpoint:* It is necessary to pinpoint explicitly the behavior that is to be eliminated or established. This takes place at many different levels relating to many differentiated behaviors. It leads to a hierarchical arrangement of skills and behaviors based upon expected specific behavioral goals. Do not deal with intangibles or ideas. If the behavior cannot in some way be both observed and measured, then you can never know if it has been either established or unlearned.

2. *Record:* List the specified behaviors in time intervals (seconds, minutes, hours, A.M., etc.) and thereby provide a precise record from which to proceed. Keep the record accurate. Do not guess; be scientific. As maladaptive responses are eliminated or decreased, more time can be devoted to more productive behaviors.

3. *Consequate:* Set up the external environmental contingencies (including primarily your own personal responses) and proceed with the program. Contingencies include approval, withdrawal of approval, disapproval, threat of disapproval, or ignoring. Reinforcement techniques may be words (spoken—written), expressions (facial—bodily), closeness (nearness—touching), activities (social—individual), and things (materials—food—playthings—money). Remember that when you ignore, behaviors often initially increase (sometimes for long periods) before they are eliminated.

4. *Evaluate:* Be prepared to stay with a program long enough to ascertain its effectiveness. Compare records after consequating with records taken before. Is the behavior increasing, decreasing, or remaining the same? Learn from your mistakes. And **"If at first you don't succeed"**—well, you know.

Being a good parent—art or science?

The question will continue to be asked, "What makes a good parent?" Analyzing a parent's behavior is really no different from analyzing children's behavior. Earlier it was stated that children must know what is expected of them and want to do it. Most parents have at least a general idea of what is expected of them and also want to be good parents. However, if they do not structure the behaviors to be learned, practice techniques of effective behavioral control, and maintain consistency, they fail. Every principle relating to a child's behavior throughout the preceding chapters also applies to parents. However, it is much more important that parents realize *it is their responsibility* to insure that proper learning actually takes place—not the child's. How easy it is for some of us to give *our* problem to someone else. "I have to stick up for my child, don't I?" "Well, if you had to sit around home all day maybe you wouldn't be consistent either." "If I didn't have to work then maybe I could spend more time with the children." "He didn't act like that before he started scouts." Perhaps extreme examples of giving the problem away is manifest by supposedly responsible parents who blame alcohol, drugs, schools, or the wrong crowd for their children's failures. The parent who really cares will persevere and have courage. Through trial and error parents will find better ways to stimulate their children toward optimum potentials. With or without a full understanding of behavioral principles, the parent will come to find better methods of behavioral control and character development.

The ability to recognize individual differences and structure a home environment with meaningful contingencies relevant to specific situations represents an outstanding accomplishment. However, good taste is also of major importance. The authors know of a parent who controlled his small children by locking them up in closets for several hours when they misbehaved, and another parent who continued to frighten her children by saying the "boogy man" would get them if they didn't close their eyes. One instructor made children participate in a mock wedding ceremony if they were very, very bad. When the children evidenced proper behaviors, they were then allowed to "get divorced." These disciplinary procedures were consistent and tremendously effective; however, they raise many serious questions regarding the acquisition of other associations. Another person told of a technique she used with eight- and nine-year-old boys. "When one of the boys misbehaves, I make him wear a girl's ribbon in his hair." Does it work? Very well; but again, we question the advisability of such insensitivity.

One mother, after having been provided with a strong positive program to get her five-year-old child to finish eating on time, returned with her husband who stated that he had vetoed her approach and put his own program in action: If the child finished eating within the time limit the child got to hit the father twice with a belt; when he didn't finish on time he got hit twice by the father. The father proudly stated that the boy was now finishing early every time and really "developing a good swing."

It is readily apparent that regardless of how many "behavioral recipes" are available, the insensitive parent will still be found wanting. The art of being a good parent seems directly contingent upon the behavior of the parent as a person. Modeling effects assimilated through the influence of an outstanding individual are still some of the most powerful and far-reaching. The truly effective parent will combine the science of behavior with the art of living to create that exceptionally rare atmosphere —an environment where children not only take excitement from discovery, but learn to be nice people.

part **2**

BEHAVIORAL PRINCIPLES APPLIED

## chapter 6

TIME
THE MEASUREMENT OF RESPONDING

Will it work with my child?

The preceding essays comprising Part I were not presented to express maverick points of view. These issues were developed to prepare the parent to deal with human behavior more objectively. It is extremely easy to make-believe, to pretend that behavior is mystical and that somehow children will learn the opposite of what they are taught. Do we readily take credit when someone compliments our children yet find "good" reasons when inappropriate behaviors are brought to our attention? If we are honest, we must take our share of the grief as well as the joy. Perhaps the most frightening aspect of parenthood is that behavior is most certainly learned, and, for this, we as parents must take full responsibility. Pretending *is* easier, for discipline is an awesome challenge. We prefer to believe that our deviant child will somehow change—that his bad behavior is just a stage, or if only he could work it out of his system everything would be all right. We hope, but hope wears thin without positive signs of improvement. We struggle, we wait, we often become discouraged, and finally we realize that it is indeed a cause-and-effect world: in the long run we do "reap that which we sow." After myths are laid aside; after we stop feeling guilty, stop worrying, and start acting; after personal beliefs, consistency, and individual responsibility are all in harmony—the parent begins to change. Subsequently, behavior becomes more predictable and effects of specific actions assured. As behavioral principles are practiced and applied, we become confident that *wrong associations can indeed be changed*. **Will it work with my child?—Yes.**

Can behavior be measured?

The most critical difference between a behavioral approach which pinpoints specific observable and measurable behaviors and other approaches to child-rearing is the keeping of behavioral records. Evaluation of any procedure instituted to induce behavioral change is virtually impossible without records. Most individuals are not content to rely upon a "feeling" concerning their bank balance, and the bank is even less likely to honor an overdrawn check because the depositor "feels" his balance is sufficient. Is it not then curious that when we deal with human beings, who are much more important than bank balances, we change rules, reinterpret contingencies, and fail to follow through because we "feel the behavior is really not that bad" or "feel" that the child *really* understands the regulations or perhaps "feel" that we may lose the child's love or respect? Measurement and specific records are crucial for accurate evaluation. The only difficulty regarding these classification procedures is that they take a little extra effort. Behavior always occurs in time intervals. If parents are to know whether a particular behavior is getting worse, better, or staying the same, the frequency of behavioral occurrences must be recorded across time and in specific time intervals. Recording procedures are not difficult; one needs only paper, pencil, and some measure of time (clock).

For example, what if undesirable behavior in a particular home is defined as yelling. Instead of children working together, they scream at each other. The first procedure would be to know precisely how much yelling is taking place (baseline—record). If this recording does not take place and the parent first takes remedial steps, then it will not be known if the undesired behavior is getting better, worse, or staying the same. It may seem that this procedure is not necessary. "Why not just tell them to be quiet and see what happens?" The problem, however, arises *in time,* i.e., a child might get quiet immediately, but in the *long run* more yelling usually occurs. Even if the yelling child stops immediately, the problem is not solved; it continues with the other children over time. To conduct this type of recording, the parent might assign a work task and then sit so as to see the children and count the number of times specific children yelled by recording these occurrences in a number of specific time intervals (ten second, thirty second, three minute, five minute, etc.). After a few days of recording the number of such behavioral occurrences on one individual or on many, the parent has some idea of the frequency of the behavior. Similarly the same basic procedure may be used by teachers, babysitters, siblings, friends, relatives, or others who are capable of counting specific behaviors. Parents may decide that arguments between siblings should be reduced. A checksheet and pencil may be placed within reach and every afternoon, from school return until supper, each argument could be counted. Following five days of recording the parents would know precisely how many arguments occur and would have a baseline to be compared with similar counting procedures after some consequence is attempted. The same basic procedure may be used for staying out late, toilet training accidents, lying, hitting, talking back, time spent on homework, watching TV, completing work tasks, reading to younger siblings, coming to dinner on time, hanging up one's clothes, mowing the yard, driving the car, getting into the refrigerator, playing in the back yard, cooperating with friends, smiling, crying, spending time by oneself, or any other conceivable behavior (appropriate or inappropriate). It is extremely important for the parent to have a record for each behavior of concern (whether the behavior is to be increased or decreased). The time these behaviors take to record does not compare to the time a parent spends repeating instructions and reminding (nagging), or even yelling and screaming. It is interesting that a mother who said she was too busy with housework to become "a accountant besides everything else I do" was observed by experimental observers to remind her four year old to follow the household rules ninety-seven times in two hours. Checklists for behaviors of any kind may be developed (see pages 41–169). This process represents nothing more than extending principles of record-keeping across time in some specific time interval (for example, twenty minutes, A.M, P.M., during evening meal, one day, one week, playtime, fifteen seconds, or other specific times).

Behavioral principles presented in previous chapters are of little use unless accurate records are kept. The chart on page 40 is intended to serve as a model for that record-keeping. Inspection of the form will reveal its easy usability. Behaviors are defined (pinpointed) and observed by simply writing down the specified behavior and then checking its occurrence during the planned recording procedure. Consequences are applied systematically (also recorded), then the behavior is again measured in order to evaluate the effect of the consequences.

It is suggested that before parents try to change a child's behavior they read through the many Pinpoints (examples of behavioral changing) contained in Part 2 paying special attention to the notes in order to more adequately consequate specific behaviors and become familiar with the use of this recording form. (Twenty-three examples of filled-in forms are placed among the Examples.)

Can Problems be measured?—Easily.

Can you give me some examples?

The following examples represent selected scientific and professional applications of behavioral change. These excerpts are presented in a manner that should be easily understood. *Scientific Applications* are summaries of scientific studies that have been published in journals or presented by researchers at scientific conventions. Sources for these reports are listed numerically and presented on pages 197–199. *Professional Applications* represent attempts of "ordinary" parents, counselors, teachers, and others to deal with specific problems. These examples are selected from the authors' files. This cryptic format does not begin to do justice to the original reports. The thoughtful reader will begin to read original scientific literature and refer to behavioral books while trying to study carefully the cause-and-effect relationships obviously evidenced in behavioral research and writing. It is important for the parent to understand the principles underlying discipline and the application of behavioral contingencies before choosing specific techniques. Processes and principles are of much greater consequence than the choice of reinforcers. When cause-and-effect relationships are fully understood, fanciful gimmicks bring enduring change.

General Observation Form

PINPOINT _____ Person(s) observed _____

Observer(s) _____ Location _____

Time of obs. _____ Desire that behavior increase decrease

I (we) will conduct _____ observations per _____ every _____ for _____
(number)   (min-hr-day)   (day-wk)   (day-wk)

before consequating takes place.

Observation interval _____ Time between obs. _____
(sec-min-hr-day)   (sec-min-hr-day)

RECORD Each occurrence of Pinpoint			CONSEQUATE Consequences following occurrence of behavior					EVALUATE Each occurrence of Pinpoint		
Date	Obs #		Date	Obs #	Approval	Dis-approval	Other	Date	Obs #	

Total = _____   Totals = _____   _____ _____   Total = _____

Obs. = _____   # Obs. = _____

Average = _____   When _____   When _____   Average = _____

Comments _____

_____

_____

_____

_____

_____

_____

(appropriate)

for _____
(time-times)

Then these approvals will follow:

a. _____

b. _____

c. _____

(inappropriate)

Then this disapproval will follow:

a. _____

Summary:

Record total _____

Evaluate total _____

Record average _____

Evaluate avg. _____

Increase _____

Decrease _____

Example 1

Pinpoint: *Older sibling striking younger child.*
(10 year old)

Record: Forty occurrences (daily recording for seven days).

Consequate: Child sent to room for ten minutes as punishment for striking; parents played with child as reward after thirty minutes of pleasant cooperative play with sibling. Parents kept "error charts" of own mistakes (inconsistencies such as parental warnings *after* hitting, attention to hitting, etc.).

Evaluate: Striking gradually decreased to zero over two weeks in direct proportion to decreases in parents' errors.

Note: If parents do not provide approval for *not* striking (reward incompatible cooperative responses) isolation may provide a good payoff for the child and striking may actually increase.

Professional Application

Example 2

Pinpoint: *Teasing other children during play.*
(individual child, 10 years old)

Record: Twenty-five occurrences which disrupted play; mother's observation for four days.

Consequate: *Isolation.* Tool shed cleaned making small isolation cubicle for child. Child sent to this "time-out place" for five minutes every time he disrupted play by teasing; praised when playing cooperatively.

Evaluate: Problem behavior steadily *decreased.* Following six isolations (three during first day) teasing behavior dropped to less than two per day.

Note: Teasing behavior was noted to produce "payoff" from three neighborhood boys (laughing, complaining, attending). Isolation can be very effective in other home situations (meals, living room, family conversations) when the children have "positive" family interactions they would prefer *not* to leave.

Professional Application

General Observation Form

PINPOINT *Hitting Johnny*   Person(s) observed *Mark*

Observer(s) *Mother, Father*   Location *Family room, outside*

Time of obs. *4:00 to 6:00 p.m.*   Desire that behavior increase / ⟨decrease⟩

I (we) will conduct **2** observations per *day* every *day* for *7 days*
    (number)   (min-hr-day)   (day-wk)   (day-wk)

before consequating takes place.

Observation interval *1 hour*   Time between obs. *5 min.*
    (sec-min-hr-day)   (sec-min-hr-day)

RECORD — Each occurrence of Pinpoint			CONSEQUATE — Consequences following occurrence of behavior					EVALUATE — Each occurrence of Pinpoint		
Date	Obs #		Date	Obs #	Approval	Dis-approval	Other (Errors)	Date	Obs #	
3/14	1	✓✓✓	3/21	1	✓	✓✓	✓✓	3/21	1	✓✓✓
3/14	2	✓✓	3/22		✓	✓	✓✓✓	3/21	2	✓✓
3/15	1	✓✓✓✓	3/23		✓✓	✓✓✓	✓✓	3/22	1	✓✓✓✓
3/15	2	✓✓	3/24		✓✓✓	✓	✓	3/22	2	✓✓
3/16	1	✓✓	3/25		✓✓	✓✓	✓	3/23	1	✓✓✓
3/16	2	✓	3/26		✓✓✓	✓	✓	3/23	2	✓✓
3/17	1	✓✓	3/27		✓✓✓	✓		3/24	1	✓✓
3/17	2	✓✓✓✓✓	3/28		✓✓✓	✓		3/24	2	✓
3/17	2	✓	3/29		✓✓✓✓		✓	3/25	1	✓
3/18	1	✓✓✓	3/30		✓✓✓	✓	✓	3/25	2	✓
3/18	2	✓✓	3/31		✓✓✓			3/26	1	✓✓
3/19	1	✓✓✓	4/1		✓✓✓		✓	3/26	2	✓
3/19	2	✓	4/2		✓✓✓	✓		3/27	1	✓
3/20	1	✓	4/3		✓✓✓			3/27	2	
3/20	2	✓✓						3/28	1–2	
								3/29	1–2	✓✓
								3/30	1–2	✓
								3/31	1–2	✓
								4/1	1–2	✓
								4/2	1–2	✓

RECORD
Total = **40**
# Obs. = **14**
Average = **2.5**

Comments *Evaluate and consequate concurrent.*

CONSEQUATE
Totals = **44**   **14**   **13**

When *Mark cooperates*
(appropriate)
for **30 min.**
(time-times)
Then these approvals will follow:
a. *play*
b. *praise*
c. ____

When *Mark hits*
(inappropriate)
Then this disapproval will follow:
a. *isolation for 10 minutes*

EVALUATE
Total = **30**
# Obs. = **28**
Average = **1.07**

Summary:
Record total **40**
Evaluate total **30**
Record average **2.50**
Evaluate avg. **1.07**
Increase ____
~~Average~~ Decrease **1.43**

General Observation Form

PINPOINT _Verbal teasing_   Person(s) observed _Jerry_
Observer(s) _mother_   Location _Backyard_
when boys play
Time of obs. _4:00 to 5:15 p.m._   Desire that behavior increase (decrease)

I (we) will conduct ___1___ observations per _day_ every _day_ for _4 days_
       (number)   (min-hr-day) (day-wk) (day-wk)
before consequating takes place.

Observation interval _1 hr, 15 min._   Time between obs. _1 day_
     (sec-min-hr-day)   (sec-min-hr-day)

RECORD Each occurrence of Pinpoint			CONSEQUATE Consequences following occurrence of behavior					EVALUATE Each occurrence of Pinpoint		
Date	Obs #		Date	Obs #	Approval	Dis-approval	Other	Date	Obs #	
10/15	1	✓✓✓✓✓✓	10/23	1	✓✓✓	✓✓✓		11/5	1	✓✓
10/16	1	✓✓✓✓	10/25	1	✓✓✓✓	✓		11/7	1	✓✓
	1	✓✓	10/26	1	✓✓✓✓	✓✓		11/9	1	✓✓✓
10/19	1	✓✓✓	10/28	1	✓✓✓			11/13	1	✓✓
10/21	1	✓✓✓✓	10/31	1	✓✓✓✓			11/18	1	✓
	1	✓		1	✓✓			11/20	1	✓
			11/2	1	✓✓✓✓✓			11/24	1	0
				1	✓✓			11/28	1	0

Total = _25_   Totals = _29_   _6_   Total = _11_
# Obs. = _4_   # Obs. = _8_
Average = _6.25_   When _Jerry cooperates_   When _Jerry teases_   Average = _1.38_
            (appropriate)   (inappropriate)

Comments _when this recurs, we should give a reward every day Jerry cooperates._

for _10 min._
(time-times)
Then these approvals
will follow:
a. _praise_
b. _____
c. _____

Then this
disapproval
will follow:
a. _isolation in tool shed_

Summary:
Record total _25_
Evaluate total _11_
Record average _6.25_
Evaluate avg. _1.38_
Increase _____
Decrease _average 4.87_

43

Example 3

Pinpoint:	*Homework study time.* (11 and 13 year olds)
Record:	Average 4.5 minutes homework per child per school day after four week's recording according to child's records. Parent's spot checks averaged 3.8 minutes.
Consequate:	Television viewing time made contingent on homework time whether or not assigned. Each minute of homework or review time redeemable for six minutes of viewing time. Children kept own time logs. Given extra monetary reward when parent's record within two minutes of child's report.
Evaluate:	Homework study time increased to thirty-two minutes per child per day at which time parents changed the study/viewing ratio to 3–1 with no decrease in study time.

Professional Application

Example 4

Pinpoint:	*"Joy riding."* (15-year-old boy)
Record:	Picked up by police on first offense.
Consequate:	Juvenile judge placed boy on probation in care of parents with charge to supply appropriate disapproval. Parents restricted boy to house except for school but purchased highly desired article to "prove they still loved him in spite of the problem."
Evaluate:	Boy continued to get in trouble—three serious instances during the next three months.
Note:	Parents inadvertently rewarded boy for getting into trouble with "love present" and boy learned that "when you do bad things, good things happen to you."

Professional Application

General Observation Form

PINPOINT *Homework Study Time*   Person(s) observed *Terry, Mary*
Observer(s) *Terry and Mary*   Location *Terry's room, Mary's room*
Time of obs. *4 to 6 p.m.*   Desire that behavior (increase) decrease

I (we) will conduct ___*1*___ observations per *week* every *week* for *4 wks.*
　　　　　　(number)　　　　　　(min-hr-day)　　(day-wk)　　(day-wk)
before consequating takes place.

Observation interval ___*3 minutes*___   Time between obs. ___*none*___
　　　　　(sec-min-hr-day)　　　　　　　　　　　(sec-min-hr-day)

RECORD — Each occurrence of Pinpoint			CONSEQUATE — Consequences following occurrence of behavior					EVALUATE — Each occurrence of Pinpoint		
Date	Obs #		Date	Obs #	Approval	Dis-approval	Other	Date	Obs #	
Mon.	Terry ✓✓		Mon.		✓✓			Wed.	Mary ✓✓✓✓	
			Tues.		✓			"	" ✓✓	
Wed.	Mary ✓		Wed.		✓✓✓			Fri.	Terry ✓✓✓	
			Thurs.		✓✓			"	" ✓✓	
Tues.	Terry ✓		Fri.		✓✓			Mon.	Terry ✓✓✓	
			Sat.		✓✓✓✓			"	" ✓✓✓	
Thurs.	Mary ✓✓✓		Sun.		✓✓			Thurs.	Mary ✓✓✓✓	
			Mon.		✓✓			"	" ✓✓✓✓	
Wed.	Terry ✓		Tues.		✓✓			"	" ✓✓	
			Wed.		✓✓			Tues.	Terry ✓✓✓✓	
Fri.	Mary ✓		Thurs.		✓✓			"	" ✓✓✓✓	
			Fri.		✓✓			Thurs.	Mary ✓✓✓✓	
Mon.	Terry		Sat.	1	✓✓✓✓			"	" ✓✓✓	
				1	✓✓✓✓			Tues.	Terry ✓✓✓✓	
Thurs.	Terry ✓		Sun.	1	✓✓✓			"	" ✓✓✓	
				1	✓✓✓			"	" ✓✓✓	
								Fri.	Mary ✓✓✓✓	
								"	" ✓✓✓	
								"	" ✓✓✓	

Total = *10*　　Totals = *43*　　　　　　　Total = *78*
# Obs. = *8*　　　　　　　　　　　　　　　　# Obs. = *8.*
Average = *1.25*　When *Terry & Mary* When ___　Average = *9.75*
　　　　　　　　　study
Comments *Set up book-type ledger after first week of consequate.*

(appropriate)　　　　(inappropriate)
for *6 minutes*　　　　Then this
(time-times)　　　　disapproval
Then these approvals　will follow:
will follow:
a. *one 30-min.*　a. ___
b. *program*

A sequence 6 minutes of observation.　c. ___

Summary:
Record total ___ *10*
Evaluate total ___ *78*
Record average ___ *1.25*
Evaluate avg. ___ *9.75*
Increase *average* *8.50*
Decrease ___
Raw score increase of 68

Example 5

Pinpoint:	*Antagonism toward mother.* (11-year-old girl)
Record:	Excellent well-behaved child at school, negative/aggressive toward mother at home. Mother bossy, negative, sassy, argumentative toward daughter.
Consequate:	Mother/daughter interacted alone. Mother ignored inappropriate behavior, praised appropriate behavior.
Evaluate:	Child's initial reaction was *increased* anger and antagonism, followed by decreases in inappropriate behavior until home interaction judged normal.
Note:	Sometimes it is only necessary to break the cycle (i.e., child being negative and aggressive followed by parent being negative and aggressive followed by increases in child, etc.). In this case the mother had to weather an initial increase on the part of the daughter (arguing appeared to be the girl's payoff).

Scientific Application

Example 6

Pinpoint:	*Overactivity.* (six boys, 9 to 13 years old, mentally retarded with low-level intelligence)
Record:	Boys observed in playroom for eight days.
Consequate:	Rewarded following thirty seconds of "quiet time" (tokens exchangeable for candy). Procedure continued thirty days; during last four days token given after forty-five seconds.
Evaluate:	Overactivity reduced 67%.
Note:	Overactivity was still substantially decreased eight days later when *no rewards* were used.

Scientific Application

Example 7

Pinpoint: *Mistreatment of animals.*
(12-year-old boy)

Record: Neighborhood adults reported to parents they had seen boy beating their dog with sticks. Child also observed putting cats under water (four occurrences in six weeks).

Consequate: Parents purchased small dog, made son completely responsible for care and feeding, including exercise. Boy paid 25¢ per day when pet was fed and exercised. When boy forgot, he fed dog before he was allowed to eat himself. No payment was made when he forgot.

Evaluate: No incidents of animal abuse during next two weeks.

Note: After the boy had cared for his pet for six weeks he stated that he did not want any money for doing it anymore because now he really "loved Rags." It seems we learn to love by doing—perhaps this helps explain why parents love their children.

Professional Application

Example 8

Pinpoint: *Garbage removal from kitchen.*
(15-year-old boy)

Record: Mother recorded reminding boy to take out garbage an average of five times prior to any action.

Consequate: If garbage not removed prior to supper, garbage can was placed on boy's chair at evening meal.

Evaluate: Entire family laughed the first time son discovered the can. Boy promptly took the can outside and returned to the kitchen. Three days later the same procedure was employed. Following six instances (during three-week period), boy decided to give himself reminder cues, constructed a sign in bedroom "empty the trash." Job completed with no relapses.

General Observation Form

PINPOINT *Garbage not taken out*   Person(s) observed *Gary*

Observer(s) *Mom*   Location *Kitchen*

Time of obs. *Suppertime*   Desire that behavior increase (decrease)

I (we) will conduct ___*1*___ observations per *day* every *day* for *5 days*
    (number)   (min-hr-day)   (day-wk)   (day-wk)

before consequating takes place.

Observation interval *Once before supper* Time between obs. *one day*
    (sec-min-hr-day)   (sec-min-hr-day)

RECORD Each occurrence of Pinpoint			CONSEQUATE Consequences following occurrence of behavior					EVALUATE Each occurrence of Pinpoint		
Date	Obs #		Date	Obs #	Approval	Dis-approval	Other	Date	Obs #	
11/5	1	✓	12/1	1		✓		12/20	1	
			12/4	2		✓				
11/6	2	✓	12/8	3		✓		12/22	2	
11/7	3	✓						12/24	3	
			12/12	4		✓				
11/20	4	✓						1/3	4	
			12/15	5		✓				
11/22	5	✓						1/6	5	
			12/18	6		✓				

Total = *5*   Totals = _____   *6*   Total = *0*

\# Obs. = *5*   When _____   When *Gary does not take out garb.*   # Obs. = *5*

Average = *1*   (appropriate)   (inappropriate)   Average = *0*

Comments _____

for _____
  (time-times)
Then these approvals will follow:
a. _____
b. _____
c. _____

Then this disapproval will follow:
a. *placed on table*

Summary:
Record total _____ *5*
Evaluate total _____ *0*
Record average _____ *1*
Evaluate avg. _____ *0*
Increase *average* _____
Decrease *1*

48

Note: In this case parents were able to remove themselves from an unpleasant disapproval and interact in joking fashion while still making it very clear the job should be completed. Similar techniques have been used for other household chores. One father put his 16 year old's dinner on a tray and placed it under her bed behind some dirty clothes. The clothes had to be removed before the dinner was obtained. With older children these consequences primarily serve as reminders.

Professional Application

Example 9

Pinpoint: *Complaining.*
                   (8-year-old girl)

Record: Complaints averaged 90% of the time following parental assignment of any task. (Do I have to now? I'm too tired. Can't I do something I want? I hate that job anyway, etc.)

Consequate: Each complaint resulted in addition of one more assigned task. Child assigned eight extra jobs first day (normal assignment two). Mother matter-of-factly stated, "I am sorry that you have to do another job, but when you complain you get one more."

Evaluate: After three days average number of extra jobs declined to one per day. Six months follow-up indicated average of 2.3 jobs per day (mother's records).

Note: Mother reported a slight relapse after three months when the girl wasn't feeling well (one day child assigned five extra jobs). Mother also reported that the girl continues to receive money for her jobs and no extra allowance. The authors concur in this philosophy as they think that money paid for getting seven days older is a very weak contingency, indeed.

Professional Application

General Observation Form

PINPOINT _Complaining_   Person(s) observed _Kathy_

Observer(s) _Mother and father_   Location _Household_

Time of obs. _3:45 to 9 p.m._   Desire that behavior increase (decrease)

I (we) will conduct ___1___ observations per _day_ every _day_ for _3 days_

(number)   (min-hr-day)   (day-wk)   (day-wk)

before consequating takes place.

Observation interval _Afternoon & evening_ Time between obs. _day_

(sec-min-hr-day)   (sec-min-hr-day)

RECORD Each occurrence of Pinpoint			CONSEQUATE Consequences following occurrence of behavior					EVALUATE Each occurrence of Pinpoint		
Date	Obs #		Date	Obs #	Approval	Dis-approval	Other	Date	Obs #	
Mon.	1	✓✓✓✓	Thurs.	1		✓✓✓		Sun.	1	✓✓
"	1	✓✓	"	1		✓✓✓		Mon.	2	
Tues.	2	✓✓✓	Fri.	2		✓✓✓		Tues.	3	✓
"	2	✓✓	"	2		✓				
Wed.	3	✓✓✓	Sat.	3		✓✓✓				
			"	3		✓✓✓				
			"	3		✓✓✓				

Total = _18_   Totals = _____ _24_ _____   Total = _3_

Obs. = _3_   # Obs. = _3_

Average = _6_   When _____   When _Kathy complains_   Average = _1_

(appropriate)   (inappropriate)

Comments _____   for _____   Then this disapproval will follow: Summary:

(time-times)   Record total _18_

Then these approvals will follow: Evaluate total _3_

a. _will be assigned an extra job_   Record average _____

a. _____   Evaluate avg. _____

b. _____   Increase _____

c. _____   Decrease _15_

50

Example 10

Pinpoint: *Littering.*
                       (12 year old)

Record: Materials not put away, ten daily (average, one week).

Consequate: Large Saturday Box instituted. Each child given responsibility for own materials, individually labeled. Materials not put away went in Saturday Box. Saturday Box opened one-half hour weekly. Only then could articles be recovered.

Evaluate: After second week of Saturday Box, littering decreased to two incidents weekly.

Note: The procedure seems effective in all situations and at all age levels. An author had to wait four days to recover important research materials placed by his wife in the family Sunday Box. Also, the amount of material not taken from the box that is allowed to remain week after week provides a good indication of its worth to the litterer. Some parents give away items left over two weeks.

Professional Application

Example 11

Pinpoint: *Talking, standing, blurting out, noisy inattention, turning around at school.*
                       (ten children in five different classrooms. Ages 6 years 8 months to 10 years 6 months. Teachers recommended most severe problem children in class.)

Record: Trained observers recorded inappropriate social behavior for six weeks. Average inappropriate behavior was 72%.

Consequate: Teachers: (1) made classroom rules explicit; (2) ignored behaviors which interfered with learning or teaching unless dangerous; (3) used withdrawal of approval as punishment; (4) gave praise and attention to behaviors which facilitated learning; and (5) attempted to reinforce prosocial behaviors *incompatible* with inappropriate social behaviors.

General Observation Form

PINPOINT _Littering_   Person(s) observed _Patricia_

Observer(s) _Father_   Location _Home_

Time of obs. _6:30–7:00 p.m._   Desire that behavior increase (decrease)

I (we) will conduct ___1___ observations per _day_ every _day_ for _7 days_
     (number)   (min-hr-day)   (day-wk)   (day-wk)

before consequating takes place.

Observation interval _30 minutes_   Time between obs. _24 hours_
    (sec-min-hr-day)   (sec-min-hr-day)

RECORD — Each occurrence of Pinpoint			CONSEQUATE — Consequences following occurrence of behavior					EVALUATE — Each occurrence of Pinpoint		
Date	Obs #		Date	Obs #	Approval	Dis-approval	Other	Date	Obs #	
12/1	1	卌 卌	12/8	1		卌 III		12/15	1	1
12/2	2	卌 卌	12/9	2		II		12/16	2	
12/3	3	卌 卌	12/10	3		III		12/17	3	
12/4	4	卌 卌 II	12/11	4		I		12/18	4	
12/5	5	卌 IIII	12/12	5		0		12/19	5	1
12/6	6	卌 卌 卌	12/13	6		I		12/20	6	
12/7	7	卌	12/14	7		I		12/21	7	1
								12/22	8	
								12/23	9	
								12/24	10	
								12/25	11	1
								12/26	12	
								12/27	13	
								12/28	14	

Total = _70_   Totals = ___   _16_ ___   Total = _4_

\# Obs. = _7_   When ___   When _Patricia_   \# Obs. = _14_

Average = _10_   _leaves things out_   Average = _.3_

Comments _Only four in two weeks. Forgot to put one toy away at Christmas._

for ___
   (appropriate)
   (time-times)
Then these approvals will follow:
a. ___
b. ___
c. ___

(inappropriate)
Then this disapproval will follow:
a. _put in Saturday Box_

Summary:
Record total _70 (1 wk.)_
Evaluate total _4 (2 wks.)_
Record average _10.0_
Evaluate avg. _0.3_
Increase ___
Decrease _9.7_ _per day_

Evaluate: Average inappropriate behavior decreased from 72% to 19.5%
                   over an eight-week period.

Note: Participating teachers were given a workshop in behavior modi-
                   fication during the experiment. Opportunities for each teacher to
                   see daily observation graphs probably helped to increase effec-
                   tiveness of the procedures. Parents may record their own graphs
                   for daily feedback on the effectiveness of any consequence.
                   Graphs displayed for children are also effective as helps in re-
                   ducing inappropriate behavior.

Scientific Application

Example 12

Pinpoint: *Failure to eat "nourishing" foods.*
                   (6-year old-girl)

Record: Mother reported continual nagging, longer periods taken to eat
                   food (finishes last at supper)—four days; refused to eat vege-
                   tables—three days in one week.

Consequate: Mother told daughter one morning (during breakfast there were
                   a few problems) that starting at noon the mother would no
                   longer say anything about eating but any food not finished
                   would be saved and that same food would be her next meal.
                   Girl didn't finish noon meal the first day; the mother presented
                   plate directly from the refrigerator after having prepared the
                   child's favorite evening meal. Girl just sat; still refused to eat.
                   Mother re-presented same meal the next morning; girl ate noth-
                   ing. That noon girl ate the old food.

Evaluate: Girl has never since refused meals. Mother later put a twenty-
                   minute time limit on eating with same contingency. Girl and
                   family are now able to eat peacefully together.

Note: This parent decided that the value of eating the food was im-
                   portant to her and that some negative consequences needed to
                   be employed. Other parents may choose to ignore non-eating.
                   Once the value decision has been made as to *what* should be
                   done and contingencies chosen, then consistency is critical. Per-
                   haps a more positive approach could have been developed by
                   rewarding eating rather than punishing non-eating.

Professional Application

General Observation Form

PINPOINT *Refusing food presented*   Person(s) observed *Kathy*

Observer(s) *Mother*   Location *Table*

Time of obs. *meals*   Desire that behavior increase (decrease)

I (we) will conduct __*3*__ observations per *day* every *day* for *3 days*
(number)   (min-hr-day)   (day-wk)   (day-wk)

before consequating takes place.

Observation interval *mealtimes*   Time between obs. *between meals*
(sec-min-hr-day)   (sec-min-hr-day)

RECORD — Each occurrence of Pinpoint			CONSEQUATE — Consequences following occurrence of behavior					EVALUATE — Each occurrence of Pinpoint		
Date	Obs #		Date	Obs #	Approval	Dis-approval	Other	Date	Obs #	
Mon.			Thurs.					Fri.		
Break	1	II	Lunch	1				Dinner	1	
Lunch	2	IIII	Dinner	2		✓				
Dinner	3	ᵀᴴᴷ II	Fri.					Sat.		
Tues.			Break.	3		✓		Brunch	2	
Break	4	I	Lunch			✓		Dinner	3	
Lunch	5	ᵀᴴᴷ III								
Dinner	6	ᵀᴴᴷ ᵀᴴᴷ III						Sun.		
								Brunch	4	
Wed.								Dinner	5	
Break.	7	II								
Lunch	8	III						Mon.		
Dinner	9	ᵀᴴᴷ ᵀᴴᴷ III						Break.	6	
								Lunch	7	
Thurs.								Dinner	8	
Break.	10	III						Tues.		
								Break.	9	
								Lunch	10	

Total = __56__   Totals = _____   __3__ ____   Total = __0__
# Obs. = __10__   When _____   When *Kathy refuses to eat*   # Obs. = __10__
Average = __5.6__   __(appropriate)__   __(inappropriate)__   Average = __0.0__

Comments *Consequate this is very hard to do. Evaluate — mealtime reduced to 20 min. She eats well now!*

for _____
(time-times)
Then these approvals
will follow:
a. _____
b. _____
c. _____

Then this disapproval will follow:
a. *Same food next meal*

Summary:
Record total ____ *56*
Evaluate total ____ *0*
Record average ____ *5.6*
Evaluate avg. ____ *0.0*
Increase _____
Decrease ____ *5.6*
per day

Example 13

Pinpoint: *Fighting over toys.*
(2- and 6-year-old boys)

Record: Children fought as to who owned particular toy (four times in A.M.); mother admonished children to share.

Consequate: Program instituted to teach children: (1) ownership and (2) sharing. Children told "ownership is when a toy belongs to you, and you can do anything you want with it," and "sharing is when you let somebody else use something that belongs to you." Children given separate toys (some for John, some for Marc, some for both), again admonished to share, and praised when they did.

Evaluate: Children initially hoarded their own toys (two weeks), then began to trade (three occurrences, two days), then to share (sixteen instances over four days). Fighting over toys diminished to an average of less than one per day.

Note: Parents were "tremendously" pleased. They did have one dilemma concerning consistency when their six year old gave away his tricycle to a neighbor. Some people fail to realize that it is perhaps difficult to really "share" that which does not "belong" to a person. It has been conjectured that hoarding might be a behavior reinforced initially by having little that one actually owns.

Professional Application

Example 14

Pinpoint: *Negative comments and high intensity "screaming" among family members prior to evening meal.*
(father, mother, children ages 5, 9, 13, and 16)

Record: Thirty-minute observations prior to evening meal (five days). Average 64.3 disapproving comments (38.6 high intensity "screaming" and 8.7 accompanied by parental motor disapproval—"hitting"; 43.1 comments per day by children and 21.2 by parents).

General Observation Form

PINPOINT _fighting over toys_   Person(s) observed _John & Marc_

Observer(s) _Mother_   Location _Family room_

Time of obs. _5:30-5:30 weekdays_
10:00-12:00 Saturdays   Desire that behavior increase (decrease)

I (we) will conduct _four_ observations per _week_ every _week_ for _2 wks_.
           (number)   (min-hr-day)   (day-wk)   (day-wk)

before consequating takes place.

Observation interval _2 hours_   Time between obs. _24 hours_
          (sec-min-hr-day)   (sec-min-hr-day)

RECORD — Each occurrence of Pinpoint			CONSEQUATE — Consequences following occurrence of behavior					EVALUATE — Each occurrence of Pinpoint		
Date	Obs #		Date	Obs #	Approval	Dis-approval	Other	Date	Obs #	
Wed.	1	✓✓✓	Wed.	1	✓	✓✓		Wed.	1	✓
Thurs.	2	✓✓	Thurs.	2	✓	✓✓		Thurs.	2	✓✓
Fri.	3	✓✓✓✓	Fri.	3	✓✓	✓✓		Fri.	3	✓✓
Sat.	4	✓✓✓✓	Sat.	4	✓	✓✓✓		Sat.	4	✓
Wed.	5	✓✓	Wed.	5	✓✓✓	✓✓✓		Wed.	5	✓
Thurs.	6	✓✓	Thurs.	6	✓✓✓✓	✓		Thurs.	6	
Fri.	7	✓✓✓✓	Fri.	7	✓✓✓	✓✓		Fri.	7	
Sat.	8	✓✓✓✓	Sat.	8	✓✓✓✓	✓✓✓		Sat.	8	✓

Total = _31_   Totals = _19_   _20_   Total = _7_
# Obs. = _8_   # Obs. = _8_
Average = _3.9_   When _John & Marc share_   When _John & Marc fight_   Average = _0.9_

                  (appropriate)   (inappropriate)

Comments _I think I need to "catch them being good" more often._

for _any time_
   (time-times)
Then these approvals will follow:
a. _praise_
b. _____
c. _____

Then this disapproval will follow:
a. _admonished to share_

Summary:
Record total _31_
Evaluate total _7_
Record average _3.9_
Evaluate avg. _0.9_
Increase _____
Decrease _3.0_
           per day

Consequate: Parents decided every time anyone yelled the father would deliver severe reprimand accompanied "when appropriate" by motor disapproval (spanking).

Evaluate: Disapproving comments by children *increased* (58.6) and disapproving comments by parents increased (44.3, mostly by the father).

If at first you don't succeed

Consequate II: Timer set on kitchen stove thirty minutes before meal, anyone who engaged in quiet talk during that time received a special treat *prior* to supper. Family role-played how to ignore, disapprove, and praise quiet talk using examples from daily records. Father "caught the youngest child in quiet talk" and gave special treats during the thirty-minute period; others waited.

Evaluate II: Disapproval comments by children *decreased* (13.2 average first week and 5.6 second week). Disapproval comments by parents decreased (3.3 average first week and 1.8 second week).

Note: Loud reprimands defined as disapproval by the parents may not be disapproving. Here they served to increase the very behavior the parents were trying to control. "Modeling" also occurs; children observe parents yell and scream and in turn yell and scream. Discrimination was taught using role-playing and speaking quietly received approval (special treats and praise). Parents presented dessert prior to dinner in small segments. In this case a quiet tranquil house was valued more than a traditional eating sequence. Mother reported children did *not* lose their appetites and stated, "besides my treats are part of a well-balanced meal." The older children were told that procedures were geared to younger children and that the parents and older children would participate to "help the younger ones."

Professional Application

Example 15

Pinpoint:	*Wandering around house; "boredom."* (10-year-old boy)
Record:	Eight occurrences (one day) complaining of nothing to do.
Consequate:	Each time boy was observed "wandering around" he was instructed to sit alone at kitchen table for one-half hour. He was to continue sitting until he could devise an activity.
Evaluate:	Two weeks later, nine time at table, boy structured his own time. No other occurrences of "boredom" until fourth week.
Consequate II:	Mother instituted daily agenda forms filled out with boy's participation based upon the successful experience of past two weeks.
Evaluate II:	Successful summer. No occurrences of "boredom."
Note:	Happiness is derived from meaningful activities structured in time. Sometimes even "pleasure" must be structured.

Professional Application

Example 16

Pinpoint:	*Losing; poor sportsmanship.* (8-year-old boy)
Record:	Parents attending baseball game, noticed child throwing down bat, "pouting" because of striking out (thirteen occurrences in one game).
Consequate:	Parents withdrew child from activity (one game), instructed boy by modeling, i.e., parents verbalized good sportsmanship and practiced various situations with each parent playing different parts.
Record:	No occurrences of bat throwing, although boy got in argument with official over "called strike." Parents noticed arguing behavior greatly reinforced by comments (sometimes profane) of other parents attending game.

Consequate II:	Parents used negative adult modeling, i.e., "Wasn't that terrible of those adults to call the umpire names—aren't you glad your parents don't yell inappropriate things like that?"
Record II:	No other occurrences of arguing or bat throwing. Actual increase in describing other youngsters' unsportsmanlike conduct.
Note:	In situations regarding sportsmanship, parents must realize how parents themselves actually behave. Most child behavior is learned from modeling adults. Often parents must choose to select the adults who interact with their children. Other situations demand parents teach children to discriminate between appropriate and inappropriate adult behavior as in the above case.

Professional Application

Example 17

Pinpoint:	*Rowdiness in school.* (thirty 12 year olds)
Record:	Average of eight disruptive behaviors during each ten-second interval observed by teacher in school.
Consequate:	Students allowed play break with admonition: "I will let you play now if you promise to work afterwards." Students promised they would.
Evaluate:	*In*effective study behavior (nine to twelve average for ten-second intervals).
Note:	Rewards must come *after the fact*. After correct "work precedes play" contingency has been established, sequencing may then become effective (i.e., work, play; work, play; work, etc.).

Professional Application

Example 18

Pinpoint: *Appropriate sex role behavior.*
                         (175 boys, 85 girls; ages 5 years 10 months to 6 years 8 months)

Record: Series of ingeniously devised experimental studies recorded amount of play with same sex-typed toys as contrasted with opposite sex-typed toys or neutral toys (girls' toys included doll, pearl beads, high-heeled shoes, a mirror and play make-up materials, cups and dishes, and a baby carriage with a doll; boys' toys consisted of boxing gloves, a tank, a racing car, a sword, a gun, a catcher's mitt and a baseball; neutral toys included a pegboard, three old blocks, and three pieces of tinker toys. The neutral toys were deliberately less inviting for purposes of the experiments.)

Consequate: Peer and adult models observed by children playing with either "sex-inappropriate" or "sex-appropriate" toys. Some models gave approving or disapproving comments. For example, "I don't want to play with those; they are girls' toys." Some models said nothing while playing with toys and others gave verbal cues as well as playing. (Five separate experimental studies were completed with excellent control groups.)

Evaluate: Even with little total time exposure to models (less than ten minutes), when children saw peer and adults playing with toys, this increased time spent with toys. Children who saw models receive approval after playing with certain toys played more with these toys themselves (even when no approval given to children). Children who observed others receive disapproval for playing with certain toys tended to avoid the same toys themselves. Children who observed someone giving themselves reasons for not playing with certain toys and who did not engage in play themselves were better able to gain similar control over their own behavior.

Note: These studies are extremely important for parents who desire to increase or decrease the sex-role identity of their children. Society has changed very dramatically in the last few years, and it becomes more and more difficult to draw distinctions between masculine and feminine roles. However, parents who are concerned should label verbally and reinforce whatever they consider to be appropriate behavior from a very young age to discriminate or not discriminate differentiations which fit within the parents' value system. The above studies clearly demonstrate the cause-and-effect relationship between (1) supplying a child with the label, (2) modeling appropriate behaviors, and (3) producing same.

Scientific Application

Example 19

Pinpoint:	*Stuttering.* (three adult males)
Record:	Stuttering tabulated by analyses of two-minute intervals.
Consequate:	Stuttering resulted in mild shock delivered to wrist.
Evaluate:	Almost total reduction of stuttering. However, when shock removed, stuttering returned to original frequency.
Note:	The use of electric shock as disapproval must be carefully controlled under appropriate supervision. This single scientific application (chosen from many) merely illustrates that the job is only half done when the inappropriate behavior is not replaced with appropriate behavior.

Scientific Application

Example 20

Pinpoint:	*Inappropriate oral hygiene.* (12-year-old boy and 10-year-old girl)
Record:	Brushing done *only* at parental insistence. (Recording over two-week period.)
Consequate:	Two-track program devised: (1) Children directed (by father—one week) to brush after breakfast and dinner and "feel your teeth with your tongue and smell your own breath." (2) During second day of second week father "caught" children after observing tooth-brushing. Father said, "If you've brushed, you may open my hand and have the prize inside" (5 or 10 cents), once daily. During same week father "caught" children when brushing was omitted and said same thing, but when children said, "I haven't" the father said, "open my hand anyway and see what *you might have had.*"
Evaluate:	"Brushing" behavior amplified to operational point of acceptability (i.e., four *forgets* each week).
Note:	Children can be taught to appreciate the "good" smell of their breath as well as the "feel" of clean teeth.

Professional Application

Example 21

Pinpoint:	*Getting up during nap time.* (4-year-old boy)
Record:	Boy got up four to five times daily (average for seven days). Mother spanked child twice daily for getting up and reported constant warning called into bedroom.
Consequate:	(1) Paddled child less frequently and much harder so that it ceased being a means of attention. (2) Ignored all sounds from child; only intervened when child actually got out of bed. (3) Rewarded quiet time in bed by bringing in special treats and praising child for lying quietly: first time aften ten seconds, then fifteen seconds, then five, then thirty, then eighteen, then twenty-eight, then ten, then thirty-six, etc., gradually increasing time span with some short times in between promising child mother would come in again (building hope) each time she left. (4) After boy asleep, placed special treats on bed.
Evaluate:	After two spankings in one day plus three days of gradually taking in special little treats (variable times) boy waited quietly for rewards and fell asleep every single day.
Note:	When approval is, in fact, reinforcing to a child and is given in an unpredictable way such as the one used in this case, the child is unable to tell when the reward will be given and waits for a longer and longer time hoping the reward will come. Gradually the child will learn to tell himself how good he is behaving, if similar comments are directed toward the behavior every time the parent rewards. Severe disapproval is used to stop unwanted inappropriate behavior and an unpredictable approval schedule to teach incompatible responses (i.e., children lying quietly are not up) while building persistence in maintaining appropriate behavior.

Professional Application

General Observation Form

PINPOINT *Getting up during nap* Person(s) observed *Joe*

Observer(s) *Mother* Location *Bedroom*

Time of obs. *2:30 – 4:00 p.m.* Desire that behavior increase (decrease)

I (we) will conduct ___*1*___ observations per *day* every *day* for *7 days*
(number) (min-hr-day) (day-wk) (day-wk)

before consequating takes place.

Observation interval *1½ hours* Time between obs. *daily*
(sec-min-hr-day) (sec-min-hr-day)

RECORD Each occurrence of Pinpoint			CONSEQUATE Consequences following occurrence of behavior					EVALUATE Each occurrence of Pinpoint		
Date	Obs #		Date	Obs #	Approval	Dis-approval	Other *got up*	Date	Obs #	
2/13	1	////	2/20	1	///// /////	//	//	2/27	1	
2/14	2	/////	"	1	///// ///// //			2/28	2	
2/15	3	///// /	2/21	2	///// ///// /////	/	/	3/1	3	
2/16	4	////	"	2	///// ///// //			3/2	4	
2/17	5	////	2/22	3	///// /////			3/3	5	
2/18	6	///// /	"	3	///// ///			3/4	6	
2/19	7	/////	2/23	4	///// //			3/5	7	
			2/24	5	///					
			2/25	6	///					
			2/26	7	/					

RECORD		CONSEQUATE		EVALUATE	
Total =	34	Totals = 81	3	Total =	0
# Obs. =	7			# Obs. =	7
Average =	4.9			Average =	0

When *Joe stays in bed* (appropriate) for *5–60 seconds* (time-times) Then these approvals will follow:
a. *Treats*
b. *praise*
c. _____

When *Joe gets up* (inappropriate) Then this disapproval will follow:
a. *hard spank*

Comments *Ignore all sounds unless up – put reminders on kitchen clock for variable approvals – spanked twice – 2/25 asleep so put treat on pillow*

Summary:
Record total ___34___
Evaluate total ___0___
Record average ___4.9___
Evaluate avg. ___0.0___
Increase _____
Decrease ___34___
per wk.

63

Example 22

Pinpoint: *Thumb-sucking.*
                 (7-year-old girl)

Record: Thumb-sucking occurred 45% of time girl watched TV or
                 read (mother's records). Dentist indicated "bite" was getting
                 worse.

Consequate: Mother, after hearing P.T.A. lecture on "A positive approach
                 with record-keeping," "caught" girl every time she had thumb
                 in mouth. If thumb removed, girl received praise and special
                 checks on prominently displayed chart in living room. (Checks
                 were to be traded for bicycle-picture of bicycle at end of chart).
                 Mother continued for fourteen days.

Evaluate: Thumb-sucking *increased* to 75%. Mother sought professional
                 help from behaviorally oriented counselor stating, "I tried, but
                 bribery just doesn't work."

Note: A cause-and-effect approach rests upon record-keeping (data).
                 In this case the consequence did in fact work (changed be-
                 havior). Thumb-sucking *increased* 30%. The behavior change,
                 however, was not in the direction desired by the mother (nor the
                 dentist). Regarding the "bribery" issue, some parents confuse
                 the use of approval with a notion of "bribery." The girl in this
                 case learned exactly what she was taught—(1) put thumb in
                 mouth, (2) take thumb out of mouth, and (3) get rewarded.
                 The girl was rewarded for what she was not supposed to do. The
                 parents must be careful not to reinforce the child by making a
                 "deal" *after* the misbehavior has occurred or *after* the time for
                 something to be done has passed. "If you stop dawdling and do
                 the dishes, I'll give you a dime," teaches dawdling. "Stop fight-
                 ing, and you'll get some ice cream," teaches fighting. "If you
                 stop that arguing, then I'll let you take the car," teaches argu-
                 ing for the car. "If you stop that screaming in the store, I'll give
                 you some soda pop," teaches screaming for stopping. In each
                 instance children are given approval to *stop* inappropriate be-
                 havior but actually learn to *begin* the inappropriate behavior so
                 they can make a "deal" to stop so they can get a reward (gen-
                 erally on a partial schedule as we don't give in every time, and,
                 thus, the child also learns persistence in misbehavior). Parents
                 should either use ignoring or disapproval to stop or extinguish
                 the misbehavior. Teaching for incompatible responses using a
                 positive approach involves setting up the reward beforehand.
                 Keep your thumb out of your mouth for fifteen minutes, then
                 you get a check. I'll set the timer and if the dishes are done in
                 thirty minutes, you'll get a dime. If you play this afternoon co-
                 operatively and don't fight, I'll take you out for ice cream. If you

talk nicely when you are home for four nights, then you may take the car.

Professional Application

Example 23

Pinpoint: *"Show-off" at school.*
                   (8-year 8-month-old boy)

Record: Three specific behaviors approved by peers. Out of seat twenty times per day, talking without permission eighteen times per day, five incomplete assignments (one week).

Consequate: Program initiated retaining approval from peers. Instead of receiving laughter for getting out of seat and talking, child allowed to tell jokes; instead of receiving attention for misbehaving, child received praises for proper behavior. Boy stayed after school as reward rather than punishment.

Evaluate: First week, talking decreased to two occurrences, left seat only once. Second through fourth week *no* rules broken. Only one inappropriate behavior in fifth week.

Note: A great deal of "show-off" behavior is maintained by peer attention. If parents just remove one child from the group this often solves the problem.

Scientific Application

Example 24

Pinpoint: *Temper tantrums at bedtime.*
                   (21-month-old boy)

Record: Crying and screaming when parents left room or even read
                   while in room before child went to sleep. Tantrums occurred
                   every night unless parents spent between one-half and two hours
                   in room. (Child had been seriously ill for eighteen months re-
                   quiring extensive attention.)

Consequate: Parents gave verbal and contact affection at bedtime prior to
                   placing child in bed. Placed child in bed in a relaxed manner,
                   then left room and closed door.

Evaluate: Boy screamed continually for forty-five minutes first night; by
                   tenth night child no longer whimpered or fussed when parent
                   left room; child observed smiling in his bed.

Note: When aunt was putting child to bed following procedures, he
                   screamed and his aunt reentered the room and remained until
                   he was asleep. The second siege of screaming, crying, and
                   whimpering reached zero by the ninth night following this well-
                   intentioned "error of reinforcement." Two year follow-up re-
                   vealed no further bedtime tantrums. Consistency *is* difficult.

Scientific Application

Example 25

Pinpoint: *Toilet training.*
                   (19-month-old child)

Record: Mother removed restraining devices, placed child on toilet fol-
                   lowing dry naps and dry periods during day, but no successful
                   eliminations occurred. Child began to react with crying after
                   being placed on toilet four times per day for two days (mother
                   sought help as extended road trip was approaching).

Consequate: Mother placed child on toilet, entertained infant, but allowed
                   child to leave when he desired. Mother instructed to play with
                   child for longer and longer periods to help insure successful

completion of the appropriate behavior in the appropriate place (warm pan on lap with water toys also helped). When behavior occurred while still on toilet the mother:

(1) lavishly praised, especially for being "big"

(2) explained that when you "go" candy will be given

(3) explained that it would be very nice to tell Mommy or Daddy *before* you have to "go."

Evaluate: Second training session ended in success; fourth day child verbalized contingency; fifth day child went to parent followed by successful completions. Following fifteenth day candy was given only when requested. Parents satisfied that child trained. Auto trip of five days completed without accidents. Follow-up showed one short relapse for defecation only during an illness at twenty-one months with retraining successful in five days.

Note: Use of desired approval techniques led to rapid training and allowed mother to assume positive role. Spontaneous decrease in requests for candy and modeling of adult self-responsible behaviors indicates that motivation probably gets "in" more rapidly when any program is structured rather than haphazard. (*See* Example 77.)

Scientific Application

Example 26

Pinpoint: *Fear of going to school.*
(fifty children—ages 4 to 16)

Record: All children frightened of going to school, referred to University Human Development Clinic over eight-year period and had at least *seven* of the following ten behaviors: (1) first episode of school fear, (2) begun on Monday following an illness previous Thursday or Friday, (3) had begun with no warning, (4) more prevalent in lower grades (forty of fifty children were age twelve or under), (5) mother ill or presumed so by child, (6) child expressed concern about death, (7) parents communicate well, (8) mother and father happy and adjusted in most areas, (9) father shows interest in household management and problems, (10) parents easy to work with (school, church, clinic, etc.).

Consequate: Parents ignored bodily complaints (did not reinforce child's talk about feeling sick), merely made appointment with pediatrician for a time *not* during school hours or, if necessary, a quick examination on way to school. Child was taken to school usually by father with school personnel instructed to keep child in room when parents left. Parents were told that child's difficulty transient, informed Monday would be difficult, Tuesday better, and by Wednesday, problem generally absent. Parents told not to discuss school attendance over weekend (most referrals late in week). Sunday night parent stated, "tomorrow you go back to school," and discussion attempts were ignored. Monday morning child was dressed and given a light breakfast (nausea generally existed). No questions were asked about fear (parents therefore did not reinforce fear). Monday evening parents gave approval for going to school *and* staying at school (no matter how many times child cried, vomited, or tried to leave). Child also often seen briefly and explained advantages of going on in face of fear (getting right back on a horse after a fall, etc.).

Evaluate: All fifty cases responded with complete elimination of school fear. All cases followed for at least two years with no recurrences of fear.

Note: Any inappropriate behavior of recent duration with an acute onset is probably best handled immediately. Talking about the problem merely serves to intensify and prolong the behavior by giving a great deal of approval as well as reinforcing procrastination. The time to talk is after something has been done to change. *Talk should not take the place of action.* Of course, where any medical problems may be indicated careful examination is mandatory but should be handled by parents matter-of-factly. Most parents are perfectly capable of handling this type of school fear themselves. Should problems develop you think extremely severe, then seek professional help immediately.

Scientific Application

Example 27

Pinpoint:
School vandalism.
(13 year olds)

Record:
Seven students wrote on or destroyed: (1) desks, (2) walls, and (3) school equipment.

Consequate:
(1) Students sanded and revarnished damaged desks, plus two others. (2) Students washed *entire* wall. (3) Students contributed double financial value of damaged school equipment. All work strictly supervised and completed to satisfaction of teacher. Thereafter, students responsible for property upkeep, regardless of who caused damage. Parents *not allowed* to contribute to restitution in any manner.

Evaluate:
Vandalism eliminated. Students' supervision of school property established.

Note:
This is perhaps one of the oldest and most effective discipline procedures.

Professional Application

Example 28

Pinpoint:
Discriminating rules for visiting children—grandparents.
(thirteen children, 2 to 9 years old)

Record:
"Total bedlam" (three visits from other children) reported by one parent who said, "If I have to put up with those neighbor's children again, I'll even stop letting their parents visit." Another parent, "I can't do anything with that child after she comes home from Grandmother's."

Consequate:
Difficult program to teach parents to have enough courage to enforce own rules with other children and also with visits to grandparents. *Simple* program to teach visiting children discriminations. "In this house you must follow (different) rules." Visiting children told when entered house about expectations and consequences: "If you play nicely, you may have a treat, and if you break our rules (carefully explained), you must leave."

	Own children told "when we are home from grandparents' we have different rules."
Evaluate:	Children learned to discriminate (rowdy, undisciplined, only in situations where allowed) and followed rules in orderly house after being sent home twice (average) first week. Own children took average of one day to "shape up" after visit to grandparents.
Note:	Only adults' behavior presents problems in these situations. However, an initial strong positive approach with other parents, especially one's own, usually solves the problem. When adults do set strong limits with neighbor's children (especially if they pay-off from time to time, children's good behavior), their house will usually be the one all the children "love to visit." When grandparents visit it is wise to give them a set of the child's rules when they arrive, making sure to correct grandparents' deviations immediately and gently.

Professional Application

Example 29

Pinpoint:	*Fear of loud noises.* (4-year-old boy)
Record:	Loud noises of any variety started uncontrolled screaming, running around house in unpredictable fashion.
Consequate:	Behavioral therapist tried visual imagery and deep relaxation to reduce fear; was not successful. Therapist continued relaxation but added other procedures. First he would relax boy then pop balloons, drop wood, starting softly then with ever-increasing intensity. Parents presented noises at home while boy very relaxed. Father also took son to pistol practice range. Boy would lie down at distance and relax while father would go to shoot. Father moved boy progressively closer until he finally shot gun himself.
Evaluate:	Treatment discontinued after six sessions. Parents reported boy no longer afraid. Follow-ups of one month and four months showed no further problem.

Note: When dealing with some severe problems, professionals have
                   substantiated the necessity to change behavior in the situation
                   where the behavior is a problem. Many children act very well in
                   treatment offices with little or no transfer to home; many are
                   good at school and not at home or vice versa. To be effective
                   behavioral management sometimes requires an analysis of the
                   various ecological systems (home, school, neighborhood, church,
                   gang, etc.) as well as the specific payoffs which keep the be-
                   havior going.

Scientific Application

Example 30

Pinpoint: *Bed-wetting (enuresis).*
                   (forty-seven children, ages 4 through 16)

Record: Average of five nights per week including all age groups.

Consequate: Two-fold program: (1) To teach child to take responsibility
                   for own bed-wetting behavior and (2) train child to wake up
                   when the bladder pressure is high just prior to urination. Par-
                   ents purchased a simple battery operated device which consists
                   of a battery case with speaker and two leads that attach to two
                   flexible metal sheets placed on the bed separated by thin pourous
                   paper sheets. (Available fairly inexpensively through Sears,
                   Roebuck & Co.) When the urine passed through the sheet it
                   closed the circuit (no chance occurred for electrical shock as the
                   circuit was both low amperage and low voltage) and rang the
                   buzzer which awakened the child whereupon he went to the bath-
                   room. When accidents occurred the child changed his own bed-
                   ding, clothing, and helped reset the alarm. (Depending on child's
                   age, the procedures are done alone or with help of parents.)
                   Most parents also placed charts in bedroom with prizes to be
                   given after two, six, nine, fifteen, eighteen, twenty-one, and
                   thirty dry nights.

Evaluate: Forty-four children eliminated or decreased bed-wetting to one
                   accident within thirty days of starting the procedure.

Note:

When using such procedures, many parents make the mistake of limiting the child's liquid intake. This is detrimental in two ways: the acid percentage of the urine will increase and may induce urination, but more importantly the child cannot learn to "get up" with bladder pressure unless bladder pressure is increased. The buzzer procedure is built upon the principle that the child will learn to respond to internal physiological cues (increased bladder pressure) and awakening will occur earlier and earlier in the sequence until the awakening will precede the buzzer whereupon the problem will be solved. Therefore, it is important for the parent to give as much liquid as possible just before bedtime and for most efficient use also to give as much liquid as possible every time the buzzer awakens the child. It is also important for the child to wake up to the buzzer *before* the learning procedure is employed. Put the child to bed and wait until sleep is deep, start the buzzer, leave it sounding and make certain the child is awake (sometimes with "sound" sleepers ice on the stomach is effective), have child go to the bathroom (do not take hands or lead him), simulate or actually engage in urination, and then let him go back to bed himself, after which the buzzer is turned off and reset. Continue this wake-up routine until you are certain that the buzzer *always* wakes up the child (generally this takes between three and twenty-four experiences). Next give increased liquid, send the child to bed, and wait for the buzzer. (It was found that with seven children increased liquid intake and wake-up procedure alone resulted in termination of bed-wetting.)

We recommend waiting until children are at least three years old or old enough to get themselves to and from the bathroom before this routine is begun.

Should parents not have the monetary resources to purchase the buzzer, another routine built upon the same principles may be employed. The child is given increased liquid and the parents awaken the child after approximately 120 minutes. Should urination occur prior to this time wake the child up on an earlier schedule. The child should go to the bathroom by himself, drink as much liquid as possible, go back to bed, and be awakened in another 120 minutes. This should be repeated every two hours all night for seven days. (The idea is the same as above; that is, insure the bladder is full and awaken the child.) Next the parents should increase the time before waking up the child by fifteen minutes (two hours and fifteen minutes) for the next seven days and add fifteen more minutes each week until the child gets up by himself. A good physical exam should precede any application of the above routines, but parents should not worry about any special significance concerning bed-wetting. Getting up to go to the bathroom behavior is learned just like any other behavior. If it has not been learned or the learning has been slow, then we should assume the child deserves to be taught.

Professional Application

Example 31

Pinpoint: *Writing vulgar words.*
(8- and 9-year-old neighborhood boy and girl)

Record: Two letters found by parents within one week; eight vulgar words written by boy, six by girl.

Consequate: Parents talked to parents of boy. Boy's parents said, "You know kids nowadays, what can you do." Parents talked to daughter, explained proper time and place for verbal sexual discussion. Girl received special toys for bringing home notes.

Evaluate: Girl brought home four notes passed to her by same boy during next week. Wrote no more answers.

Note: Parents do not control all possible sources of reinforcement. Following the first week parents discussed notes brought home, indicated girl should ignore any note-passing behavior, and after initial time also spent time role-playing how to ignore note-passing behavior.

Professional Application

Example 32

Pinpoint: *Control of children's food intake.*
                       (sixteen children, 4 years old, enrolled in nursery school)

Record: Each child given tray with four paper cups of foods—carrots,
                       apples, celery, raisins—for morning snack. Children sat in
                       group, ate while teacher told them stories. Amounts consumed
                       recorded. Most children exhibited definite stable intakes on sev-
                       eral foods; each child knew at least names of foods.

Consequate: Three children selected for verbal approval, invited to puppet
                       playroom. Puppet talked to child; asked child to state names of
                       goods child ate for snack. Puppet had child guess food names;
                       when food previously chosen by experimenter verbalized, pup-
                       pet gave child a trinket. Sometimes light on puppet stage turned
                       off; only correct response brought it back on.

Evaluate: Increase in food consumed on first day of verbal approval.

Scientific Application

Example 33

Pinpoint: *Lying to father.*
                       (12-year-old boy)

Record: Observed incident of mishandling church property at young peo-
                       ple's social reported by minister. Boy denied doing it when his
                       father confronted him.

Consequate: Father terminated conversation, refused to communicate with
                       boy because of his lie—not the deed (boy required to refurbish
                       damaged furniture). Father talked only through mother, and
                       mother talked to child. In this fashion mother continually re-
                       lated messages, reaffirmed seriousness of lying, also talked to boy
                       about how he could get his father to believe him. One day,
                       while on ride with family, father asked who wanted ice cream.
                       All replied affirmatively including the boy. Father told mother
                       he believed other children (one younger, one older), but he did
                       not believe Jerry. Father purchased ice cream for all except

Jerry. During next six days father questioned almost every statement and took actions contrary to the desires of the boy.

Evaluate: Boy became quite upset during the course of the week, asked his father to be forgiven, told his mother he hadn't realized how important honesty was. No known instances of lying repeated.

Note: *Withdrawal of approval* is not effective unless the value of approval has previously been established. Had this father generally been disapproving over the years, withdrawing his communication would have no effect.

Professional Application

Example 34

Pinpoint: *Defecation infrequency and irregularity.*
(3-year-old boy)

Record: Boy defecated about five days apart with much pain. Past three months defecation did not occur in appropriate place but rather under beds indoors, bushes outdoors. Problem became acute when child did not defecate once during three days and after experiencing pain waited six days with even more pain. Laxatives prescribed by pediatrician unsuccessful.

Consequate: Child seen by counselor for three sessions totaling forty-five minutes combined over period of eight days. Child quieted through play, relaxed in the session, and given a soft chant: "Mommy and Daddy want Roger to go potty all the time, but he doesn't like to, Roger doesn't like to. Everybody wants for Roger to go potty, Roger to go potty, Roger's going potty. Everybody likes Roger to go potty cause then he'll feel real good." Mother also dispensed praise and popsicle when act completed in the right place. Counselor continued in second and third short sessions to give suggestions: "Mommy and Daddy will be very happy, it would feel good and not hurt and you do want to go regularly" all of which was repeated over and over again with visions of the praise and popsicles which would be the result.

Evaluate: Defecation occurred following all three sessions; defecation re-
                 warded. Child completed one appropriate behavior per day for
                 about seventy-five days followed by praise, popsicles. One year
                 follow-up indicated 290 successful completions with no further
                 problems.

Scientific Application

Example 35

Pinpoint: *Child interfering with older child's play.*
                 (3 and 9 year olds)

Record: Six instances in three days, older child complained to parent.
                 Mother then recorded for five days—average of two to three
                 "blow-ups" per day.

Consequate: Program developed to teach older child how and when to play
                 with sibling. Older child instructed in techniques of attending
                 younger child's play for short time periods while giving approval
                 to *facilitate the complete happiness of younger child*. Rewarded
                 for *complete* attention to young child's happiness with special
                 toys, separate play periods with own age peers after twenty
                 minutes' play with brother. During separate times for older
                 child, younger child kept entirely away; not allowed to interfere.

Evaluate: No instances of annoying interactions over one week.

Note: It is important for parents to realize that unless children are
                 close in age it is difficult for each child to interact with equal
                 benefit. While it is possible for children to play *independently*
                 side by side (many times this is desirable), great disparity in
                 ages or other abilities usually necessitates that one child must
                 entertain the other if children are to be in close proximity and
                 "get along." Most parents believe that older children should es-
                 tablish these behaviors as well as derive joy from concerning
                 oneself about younger siblings. Thus, parents try to promote
                 children's "loving each other rather than fighting." Perhaps most
                 "sibling rivalry" is caused by the hours, days, weeks, months,
                 and years children actually compete with each other when left
                 at their own resources. Regardless, it is imperative that older

General Observation Form

PINPOINT *Interfering with sister* Person(s) observed *Tom & Helen*

Observer(s) *Mother and Helen* Location *Family room, Helen's room*

Time of obs. *3:30–6:30 p.m.* Desire that behavior increase (decrease)

I (we) will conduct ___1___ observations per *day* every *day* for *5 days*
(number)   (min-hr-day)   (day-wk)   (day-wk)

before consequating takes place.

Observation interval *3 hours* Time between obs. *1 day*
(sec-min-hr-day)   (sec-min-hr-day)

RECORD — Each occurrence of Pinpoint			CONSEQUATE — Consequences following occurrence of behavior					EVALUATE — Each occurrence of Pinpoint		
Date	Obs #		Date	Obs #	Approval	Dis-approval	Other *playtime*	Date	Obs #	
Mon.	1	✓✓✓	Mon.	1	✓✓✓		✓	Mon.	1	—
Tues.	2	✓	Tues.	2	✓✓✓	✓	✓	Tues.	2	—
Wed.	3	✓✓	Wed.	3	✓✓		✓	Wed.	3	—
Thurs.	4	✓✓	Thurs.	4	✓✓		✓	Thurs.	4	—
Fri.	5	✓✓	Fri.	5	✓✓		✓	Fri.	5	—

Total = *11* Totals = *12* *1* *5* Total = *0*

\# Obs. = *5*   \# Obs. = *5*

Average = *2.2* When *Helen plays with Tom* When _____ Average = *0*

Comments *One blowup when I didn't keep Tom away. Tom waited and didn't go into Helen's room before playtime.*

(appropriate) for *20 minutes* (time-times) Then these approvals will follow:
a. *Toys*
b. *play alone*
c. *special prize*

(inappropriate) Then this disapproval will follow:
a. _____

Summary:
Record total _____ *11*
Evaluate total _____ *0*
Record average _____ *2.2*
Evaluate avg. _____ *0*
Increase _____
Decrease _____ *2+ per day*

children make discriminations between when they are interacting for their own pleasure and when they interact for the pleasure of someone else. Unfortunately, some parents do not even make these discriminations and while starting out to play a game with young children end up fighting over some aspect of the game!

Professional Application

Example 36

Pinpoint:	*Disruptive classroom behavior.* (9-year-old boy)
Record:	Disruptions recorded by teacher.
Consequate:	Disruptive behaviors ignored; appropriate behavior rewarded. Boy kept after school for extreme deviations and sent home on later bus. This put child with students he did not know and withdrew peer attention. Correct behaviors reinforced by teacher praise and peer-approval (continuously in beginning, more infrequently later on). Also, job of blackboard monitor followed appropriate behavior.
Evaluate:	Disruptive behaviors initially *increased* as payoff withdrawn. After initial rise, maladaptive behaviors progressively *decreased* and were eliminated by end of third week.
Note:	Parents should expect initial increases in maladaptive behaviors when starting any new routine.

Scientific Application

Example 37

Pinpoint: *Inappropriate table approaching behavior.*
(3-year-old girl)

Record: After finishing own dinner child interrupted parent while parent was still eating. Observed for three fifteen-minute periods (three meals, disruptive behavior occurred forty times).

Consequate: Parents increased approval when child engaged in quiet play away from table. Inappropriate table approaching behavior ignored. Crying and disobedience followed by isolation (time-out, bedroom with door shut for three to five minutes after crying stopped). Contingent verbal approval given to relevant appropriate behavior. On occasion, parent left dinner table to reinforce appropriate playing behavior with closeness, touching, and material reinforcements (candy). Parents also increased "on task" interaction immediately after dinner, telling child, "It was so nice of you to play quietly while Mommy had her dinner. You were so nice, and I had such a nice dinner that now I want to play with you."

Evaluate: Inappropriate behavior decreased to five interruptions after one week.

Professional Application

Example 38

Pinpoint: *Shyness and lack of dating.*
(18-year-old boy in high school)

Record: No dates over four-month period.

Consequate: Mother and father role-played various interactions including meeting in class, asking to eat lunch together, and telephone conversations to increase more positive verbal interactions such as "I thought you would like to go out with me," as opposed to "you don't want to go out with me do you?" Boy contracted with parents to accompany friend twice weekly to local church and social events. Boy observed popular boys and identified in writ-

General Observation Form

PINPOINT _Table approaching_   Person(s) observed _Jeniene_
Observer(s) _Mother_   Location _Dinner table_
Time of obs. _Suppertime_   Desire that behavior increase (decrease)

I (we) will conduct ___1___ observations per _day_ every _day_ for _3 days_
(number)   (min-hr-day)   (day-wk)   (day-wk)
before consequating takes place.

Observation interval _About 15 minutes_   Time between obs. _24 hours_
(sec-min-hr-day)   (sec-min-hr-day)

RECORD Each occurrence of Pinpoint			CONSEQUATE Consequences following occurrence of behavior					EVALUATE Each occurrence of Pinpoint		
Date	Obs #		Date	Obs #	Approval	Dis-approval	Other	Date	Obs #	
11/1	1	ℳℳ℟℟ℳ℟℟ℳ℟℟ℳ℟℟	11/4	1	///	//		11/11	1	///
11/2	2	ℳℳℳℳ//	11/5	2	//	///		11/12	2	/
11/3	3	ℳℳℳℳ///	11/6	3	////	/		11/13	3	//
			11/7	4	////					
			11/8	5	///	/				
			11/9	6	ℳℳ//					
			11/10	7	ℳℳ///					

Total = _40_
\# Obs. = _3_
Average = _13+_

Totals = _31_   _7_

When _Jeniene plays alone_
(appropriate)
for _30 seconds_
(time-times)
Then these approvals will follow: _verbal_
a. _x contact approval_
b. _candy_
c. _play after dinner_

When _Jeniene approaches_
(inappropriate)
Then this disapproval will follow: _ignore_
a. _if cries-sent to bedroom 3-5 min. following attention_

Comments _I will reinstate con-sequences if any inappro-priate behavior recurs._

Total = _6_
\# Obs. = _3_
Average = _2_

Summary:
Record total _____ _40_
Evaluate total _____ _6_
Record average _____ _13+_
Evaluate avg. _____ _2_
Increase _____
Decrease _____ _11_
per day

ing and discussion specific behaviors followed by role-playing with parents. Boy required to smile and say "hello" to girls ten times daily and record names of girls.

Evaluate: After eight refusals (three between second and third role-playing sessions), dating started. Increased to point of work interruptions after two months.

Professional Application

Example 39

Pinpoint: *Chronic constipation.*
              (3-year-old boy)

Record: Constipation begun about three months following treatment of diarrhea problem. Suppositories had since been used.

Consequate: Mother instructed to fill bathtub with water and place highly desirable toys visible to child. Child was told that as soon as he completed his task he was to call her and then he could play in the water. Mother then left room. Prize also given for successes.

Evaluate: Fifteen days of treatment eliminated problem.

Scientific Application

Example 40

Pinpoint: *School failure.*
                     (16-year-old boy)

Record: Failed all academic subjects first half of year. Parents and teach-
                     ers unable to "motivate studying."

Consequate: School counselor developed system with parents' cooperation.
                     Every teacher signed individual *daily progress report* (one small
                     sheet) after each class. Decision of signing for appropriate so-
                     cial and academic behaviors based on teacher's criteria. Allow-
                     ance, social engagements, car privileges were contingent upon
                     number of signatures earned each day.

Evaluate: Better grades. C+ average attained for last six-week period of
                     same year.

Note: Many parents offer rewards for good grades but cannot find a
                     way to cut down the time interval so that rewards are meaning-
                     ful in motivating the student. A complete academic term is very
                     long for a student who cannot exhibit correct study patterns
                     throughout one day.

Professional Application

Example 41

Pinpoint: *Verbal recrimination, loud talking, occasional fighting.*
                     (six children, ages 3 to 14)

Record: Whenever two or more children attempted to play games or in-
                     teract together for over ten minutes some negative disapproval
                     comment or fight took place (mother recorded sixteen—daily
                     average from school to suppertime). Previous method of deal-
                     ing with problem assessed "who was at fault." This generally
                     trying on children as well as parent and encouraged more argu-
                     ing except with one more participant—the parent.

Consequate: When children together in family room for approximately ten or
                     more minutes, mother suddenly announced "good family party"
                     with special prizes lasting approximately five minutes. When-

General Observation Form

PINPOINT *F's on report card*   Person(s) observed *Stan*

Observer(s) *Father*   Location *Written card*

Time of obs. *every 6 weeks*   Desire that behavior increase decrease

I (we) will conduct ___3___ observations per *6 wks.* every *6 wks.* for *18 wks.*
      (number)   (min-hr-day)   (day-wk)   (day-wk)

before consequating takes place.

Observation interval *looking at card*   Time between obs. *6 weeks*
      (sec-min-hr-day)   (sec-min-hr-day)

RECORD — Each occurrence of Pinpoint			CONSEQUATE — Consequences following occurrence of behavior					EVALUATE — Each occurrence of Pinpoint		
Date	Obs #		Date	Obs #	Approval a b c	Dis-approval	Other MONEY PAID	Date	Obs #	
6 wks.	1	卌 ll	1/21	1	✓		$ .40	24 wks.	1	卌 l
			1/28	2	✓ ✓		1.20			
12 wks.	2	卌 ll	2/4	3	✓		1.60	30 wks.	2	ll
			2/11	4	✓ ✓		2.00			
18 wks.	3	卌 ll	2/18	5	✓ ✓		2.85	36 wks.	3	—
			2/25	6	✓ ✓ ✓		4.75			
			3/4	7	✓		2.55			
			3/11	8	✓ ✓ ✓		4.40			
			3/18	9	✓ ✓ ✓		4.75			
			3/25	10	✓ ✓ ✓		4.75			
			4/8	11	✓ ✓ ✓		4.75			
			4/15	12	✓ ✓ ✓		4.75			
			4/22	13	✓ ✓ ✓		4.75			
			4/29	14	✓ ✓ ✓		4.75			
			5/6	15	✓ ✓ ✓		4.75			
			5/13	16	✓ ✓ ✓		4.75			
			5/20	17	✓ ✓ ✓		4.75			
			5/27	18	✓ ✓ ✓		4.75			
			6/3	19	✓ ✓ ✓		4.75			

Total = 21   Totals = 15 15 18 $72.00   Total = 8

\# Obs. = 3   \# Obs. = 3

Average = 7   When *Stan gets 36 signatures*   When _____   Average = 2 2/3

Comments *10¢ per signature per day 25¢ if all 7 sign each day — 3/11 he missed a signature and felt bad about it.*

(appropriate)

for *each wk.*

(time-times)

Then these approvals will follow:

a. *car on Sat.*

b. *friends on Fri.*

c. *friends in on Sun.*

(inappropriate)

Then this disapproval will follow:

a. _____

Summary:

Record total ___21___

Evaluate total ___8___

Record average _____

Evaluate avg. _____

Increase _____

Decrease *none last term*

83

ever two or more children fought no questions were asked concerning who was to blame, yet all concerned immediately lost privilege to be in family room (any toy involved was put up immediately and children sat on chairs in living room alone). Whenever two sets of children interacted separately and one set was sent to chairs, mother used opportunity to announce a "good family party" for children behaving appropriately. Procedure lasted four weeks.

Evaluate: Family group began to discipline themselves. Mother observed children's verbal comments imploring caution. Children learned to solve disagreements softly and without fighting; family disruption dropped (zero to one per day).

Note: The mother in this study enjoyed more free time and reported that family communication increased greatly as a result of "good family parties." The family also instituted a family night program where family members took charge of games, refreshments, and gave parts on program (puppet show, plays, role-playing school, and even satires on their former behavior and responses from parents).

Professional Application

Example 42

Pinpoint: *Reading "bad" literature.*
(10-year-old child)

Record: No instance of child reading "classic child stories" or factual book in two months.

Consequate: Parent paid child 1 ¢ per page to read any book in family library. Child could take the $1.00 after 100 pages or buy any book of choice for 25 ¢.

Evaluate: Child read sixty-two pages of child's encyclopedia first week; thereafter, averaged approximately fifty pages per week from "good" books. Four month follow-up indicated reading rate also increased. Child "hooked" on scientific book series.

Note: The child in this study kept the records personally. Completion of each 100 pages was countersigned by mother and presented to father for payment on a check-type book which became very important to the child.

Professional Application

Example 43

Pinpoint: *Child asks about sex.*
(eighteen children, 4 to 7 years old)

Record: Children asked parents but exhibited no factual information—a few "inappropriate" responses when questioned (parent's self-report).

Consequate: Program instituted to teach:
(1) physiological functions with appropriate pictures from encyclopedia and other appropriate sources,
(2) appropriate scientific terminology from same,
(3) "improper terminology," i.e., language used in different settings and by various subgroups to describe similar processes,
(4) value indoctrination, i.e., placing all the above within the value orientation of parents.

Evaluate: Factual information concerning sex verbalized; identification and discrimination concerning use of various words within proper context (at least four occurrences for each child over two-week periods).

Note: Perhaps the biggest reason we censor is that we do not take time to teach. One very effective teaching device is the drive-in theater where parents can turn the sound off or down and describe what is happening on the screen in a manner conducive to their child's understanding and their own value system. This is especially effective with "restricted movies." If parents believe their children will never have to understand some of these situations, perhaps they will choose not to do this. It is important that parents realize their own non-verbal behaviors regarding sex will be communicated to children regardless of what they say.

Professional Application

General Observation Form

PINPOINT *Using proper sex terms* Person(s) observed *Betty (5 yrs, 3 mos.)*
Observer(s) *father and mother* Location *any place, any time*
Time of obs. *any time* Desire that behavior (increase) decrease

I (we) will conduct ___*1*___ observations per *day* every *day* for *10 days*
  (number) (min-hr-day) (day-wk) (day-wk)

before consequating takes place.

Observation interval *24 hours* Time between obs. *sleep time*
  (sec-min-hr-day) (sec-min-hr-day)

RECORD Each occurrence of Pinpoint		✓=asks X=uses proper term	CONSEQUATE Consequences following occurrence of behavior					EVALUATE Each occurrence of Pinpoint		✓=asks X=proper term
Date	Obs #		Date	Obs #	Approval	Dis-approval	Other	Date	Obs #	
Sun.	1	✓	Sat.	1	—			Sun.	1	✓X
Mon.	2	—	Sun.	2	—			Mon.	2	X
Tues.	3	—	Mon.	3	///			Tues.	3	—
Wed.	4	✓✓✓	Tues.	4	※/			Wed.	4	X✓X
Thurs.	5	✓✓	Wed.	5	※ ※/			Thurs.	5	—
Fri.	6	—	Thurs.	6	///			Fri.	6	—
Sat.	7	—	Fri.	7	※//			Sat.	7	✓XX
Sun.	8	—	Sat.	8	///			Sun.	8	X✓X
Mon.	9	—	Sun.	9	///			Mon.	9	XXX
Tues.	10	✓✓✓	Mon.	10	/			Tues.	10	—
Wed.	11	✓✓	Tues.	11	—			Wed.	11	X
Thurs.	12	✓✓✓	Wed.	12	—			Thurs.	12	X✓X
Fri.	13	—	Thurs.	13	//			Fri.	13	X
Sat.	14	—						Sat.	14	—
Sun.	15	—						Sun.	15	—
Mon.	16	✓✓						Mon.	16	XX
Tues.	17	—						Tues.	17	✓
Wed.	18	✓✓✓						Wed.	18	X✓
Thurs.	19	✓✓✓						Thurs.	19	—
Fri.	20	✓✓✓						Fri.	20	XX

RECORD:
Total = *28 X=0*
# Obs. = *20 X=0*
Average = *1.4 X=0*

Comments *10 days over — better, listen for 10 more. I think it's my problem — must start now. Not so bad now — easier for me.*

CONSEQUATE:
Totals = *39*

When *Betty asks about sex* (appropriate) for *one time* (time-times)
Then these approvals will follow:
a. *praise question*
b. *answer immediately*
c. *give right & wrong words*

When _____ (inappropriate)
Then this disapproval will follow:
a. _____

EVALUATE:
Total = *✓=7 X=20*
# Obs. = *20*
Average = *X=1.0*

Summary:
Record total _____ *0*
Evaluate total _____ *20*
Record average _____
Evaluate avg. _____
Increase _____ *20*
Decrease _____

86

Example 44

Pinpoint:	*Crawling.* (3.4-year-old girl, preschool)
Record:	Girl spent 75% of time (observed two weeks) in off-feet position. Also avoided contacts with other children and adults.
Consequate:	Nursery school teachers *ignored* girl when not standing; approached, praised, displayed interest when girl on feet. Disapproval techniques such as anger, shame, disgust, or disappointment not used.
Evaluate:	Girl stood 75% of time during first week. During second week, up as much as other children.
Consequate II:	Contingencies reversed. Teachers approved *off*-feet behavior.
Evaluate II:	First day of reversal, girl off-feet 75% of time; second day, 81.9%.
Consequate III:	Return to praise for standing.
Evaluate III:	First hour of first day, on feet 75.9%; first hour of second day, 62.7%; by second hour, 100%. *No relapses observed.*
Note:	The reader may be wondering why one would deliberately produce inappropriate behavior. In a research study, the experimenter must determine that a particular reinforcer is really causing a specific effect. In this case the reinforcer was praise; the effect, standing. When a teacher or parent is "sure" what produces a desired change this may be enough. However, the scientist must be certain. The reversal technique will be noted repeatedly in scientific investigations. From studies of this type the principles in this book are derived.

Scientific Application

Example 45

Pinpoint:	*Repeated crying.* (4-year-old boy, preschool)
Record:	Eight crying periods each morning following mild frustrations. Whenever boy cried, teachers comforted him (picked up, talked softly, held on lap, etc.).

Consequate: Boy ignored unless "real grounds" for crying; given approval for
                       self-help attempts.

Evaluate: One crying spell in five days after initial decrease.

Consequate II: Teachers again paid attention to crying (ten days).

Evaluate II: Crying almost reached original level during record phase.

Consequate III: Boy ignored when crying; given approval for self-help (ten
                       days).

Evaluate III: Crying decreased to zero and low level maintained.

Note: The cause-and-effect relationship between adult approval and
                       child behaviors is clearly demonstrated in this case.

Scientific Application

Example 46

Pinpoint: *Low frequency talking.*
                       (4-year-old girl)

Record: Verbalization occurred only during 11% of all ten-second in-
                       tervals observed (trained observers).

Consequate: Teacher attention to child contingent on talking; when child did
                       not talk, she was ignored by teacher. Child also required to an-
                       swer questions when requesting materials before receiving them
                       (materials contingent on question answering).

Evaluate: Talking increased to average 75%.

Consequate II: Teacher attention to child contingent on non-verbalization;
                       when child talked, child ignored by teacher. (Reversal of con-
                       tingencies.)

Evaluate II: Talking decreased to 6%.

Consequate III: Again teacher gave attention for verbalizations, but stopped re-
                       quiring talking before providing requested materials.

Evaluate III: Child's talking increased to 61%, dropped to 28% when ques-
                       tioning and further talking eliminated.

Note: Authors indicate that since talking dropped when teacher discontinued the questioning as requirement for receiving materials, it is clear that it was not the teacher's social approval alone that was responsible for the high rate of talking. They report that questioning the child and requiring several responses before allowing access to materials is crucial. Many parents are prone to give the child what he wants without requiring much verbalization or taking the time to teach proper speech patterns. In fact, some parents actually model inappropriate speech (baby talk) without taking into consideration the disservice they provide to their child.

Scientific Application

Example 47

Pinpoint: *Nail biting, chewed fingernails.*
                      (eighteen individual children, ages 5 through 21)

Record: Excessive nail biting as evidenced by fingers. One instance of physical damage.

Consequate: *Negative practice.* Practice inappropriate behavior at specific times (e.g., 8:00 A.M. for five minutes) in front of mirror. Parent, teacher, peer, brother, or sister delivered disapproval responses during nail-biting sessions: "Doesn't that look terrible? Do you want people to see you bit your nails like that?" Children instructed to move hand up and down, biting repeatedly. During first session six children cried and wanted to stop.

Evaluate: Nail biting ceased after six to twelve sessions.

Note: Behaviors such as nail biting are behaviors whose frequency has made them habitual. Concentrated negative practice probably serves as a stimulus by which the child begins to discriminate. The child learns to "think" as his hand starts to go up, and therefore inhibits himself. Negative practice has been used successfully in eliminating nose-picking, thumb-sucking, public scratching, tics, and other social improprieties.

Professional Application

General Observation Form

PINPOINT _Chewed off nails_   Person(s) observed _Tracy_

Observer(s) _Father_   Location _Living room_

Time of obs. _Weekly inspection_   Desire that behavior increase (decrease)

I (we) will conduct _____1_____ observations per _week_ every _week_ for _4 wks_
          (number)   (min-hr-day)   (day-wk)   (day-wk)

before consequating takes place.

Observation interval _one minute_   Time between obs. _7 days_
                              (sec-min-hr-day)   (sec-min-hr-day)

RECORD Each occurrence of Pinpoint			CONSEQUATE Consequences following occurrence of behavior					EVALUATE Each occurrence of Pinpoint		
Date	Obs #	0=chewed −=ok	Date	Obs #	Approval	Dis-approval	Other 10 MINS BITING	Date	Obs #	0=chewed −=ok
7/12	1	Lt 00000	8/3	1		7HL 7HL 11	✓	8/23	1	Lt − − − − −
		Rt 00000	8/4	2		7HL 111	✓			Rt 0 − 00 −
7/19	2	Lt 0 0000	8/5	3		7HL 7HL 1	✓	8/30	2	Lt − − − − −
		Rt 00000	8/6	4		7HL 7HL 11	✓			Rt − − 00 −
7/26	3	Lt 00000	8/7	5		7HL 7HL 1	✓	9/6	3	Lt − − − − −
		Rt 00000	8/8	6		7HL 111	✓			Rt − − − − −
8/2	4	Lt 00000	8/9	7		7HL 1111	✓	9/13	4	Lt − − − − −
		Rt 00000	8/10	8	PARTY AT HOME					Rt − − − − −
			8/11	9		7HL 7HL 11	✓✓	9/20	5	Lt − − − − −
			8/12	10		7HL 7HL 11	✓			Rt − − − − −
			8/13	11		7HL 1111	✓			
			8/14	12		7HL 7HL 11	✓			
			8/15	13		7HL 7HL 11	✓			
			8/16	14		7HL 7HL 7HL	✓			

Total = _40_   Totals = _____   _143   14_   Total = _5_

Obs. = _4_   _____   # Obs. = _5_

Average = _10_   When _____   When _Tracy bites_   Average = _1.0_

Comments _____

          (appropriate)   (inappropriate)   Summary:

for _____   Then this   Record total _40_

          (time-times)   disapproval   Evaluate total _5_

Then these approvals   will follow: Record average _10_

will follow: a. _Recite comments from list_   Evaluate avg. _1.0_

a. _____   Increase _____

b. _____   Decrease _to zero_

c. _____

Example 48

Pinpoint:	*Isolate behavior.* (4.3-year-old girl)
Record:	Varied repertory of well-developed skills pleased adults but did not gain child-child interactions. Observations during entire mornings by trained observers (one week) indicated 10% child interaction, 40% adult interaction, 50% isolate.
Consequate:	Maximum adult attention for child interaction. *No* attention for isolate behavior or adult interaction.
Evaluate:	Over six days child interaction increased to 60%; adult interaction decreased to 20%; time spent alone, 20%.
Consequate II:	Contingencies withdrawn.
Evaluate II:	Child interaction *decreased* to 20%; adult interaction *increased* to 40%; isolate 40%.
Consequate III:	Contingencies reestablished. Attention for interaction with children. Child interaction increased to 60%; adult decreased to 25%; 15% isolate.
Note:	Follow-up observations showed girl to be maintaining increased ratio of child interaction.

Scientific Application

Example 49

Pinpoint:	*Inappropriate restaurant behavior.* (early experiences, sixteen children)
Record:	Parents indicated difficulty of young children to "sit still in restaurant" (parents' self-report).

Consequate:	Parents told to:
	(1) insure child is hungry before going to restaurant
	(2) explain rules to children
	    (a) we sit on our chair and talk with "inside voices"
	    (b) we use utensils for eating
	    (c) if we make loud noises *dinner is ended.*

Evaluate: All sixteen children learned to eat with decorum in restaurants but only three did *not* have to be taken out at least once during the learning phase.

Note: Parents must be certain that they are willing to take child out immediately, when necessary, and perhaps lose part of a meal themselves. Parents should make sure that only one person in family takes out the misbehaving child and all others stay and at least simulate finishing the meal. Parents also are instructed to make certain that only one warning is given; the second time the behavior is evidenced, the child should be quietly removed while the parent repeats how sorry he is that the child was not "responsible." Parents also are instructed to point out both good and bad models in the restaurant to increase discrimination between appropriate and inappropriate behavior. It is also useful to play restaurant at home two or three times before going out in public. This positive approach can be used for many public places but is generally just opposite to what most parents do. Many parents pay attention to the child only when misbehavior occurs, are not willing to leave without their own food, yet wonder why children "can't sit still."

Professional Application

Example 50

Pinpoint: *Unfinished assignments, bothering neighbors, playing in class.* (two 2nd grade boys, referred by teacher)

Record: Trained observers recorded average of 47% inappropriate behavior.

Consequate: Teacher and class formulated rules. Rules repeated six times per day for two weeks.

Evaluate: Little decrease in inappropriate behavior (average 40%).

Note: Apparently just knowing (being able to repeat rules) is not effective.

Consequate II: Teacher attempted to ignore inappropriate behaviors (teacher not entirely successful). Continued to repeat class rules every day.

Evaluate II: Behavior worsened. Average inappropriate behavior for four observations was 69%.

Consequate III: Teacher praised prosocial behavior, repeated classroom rules, ignored inappropriate behavior.

Evaluate III: Inappropriate behavior *decreased* (average of 20%). Combination of procedures effective in reducing inappropriate behavior.

Consequate IV: Teacher instructed to act as she had in September. (Observers monitored entire year.)

Evaluate IV: Inappropriate behavior increased same day teacher changed (average 38%).

Consequate V: Rules, ignoring, and praise reinstated for remainder of school year.

Evaluate V: Inappropriate behavior again decreased (averaged only 15% for last eight-week period.)

Note: Many teachers and parents who believe they use more approval than disapproval do not do so when monitored by trained observers. It is necessary to practice delivering responses and to give yourself time cues, buzzer cues, or cues written on material you are working around (kitchen cupboard sign). The sign can remind you to "catch someone being good." It is interesting to note that one boy reported in this study was seen during the entire year by a professional counselor. This boy responded in the same way to consequences as did another boy who was not seen. It would seem that teachers and parents are capable of handling many behavioral problems generally referred to counselors, if responses are well-developed and applied contingently. Remember to keep a record (perhaps under the sign taped to the cupboard) of how often approval and disapproval comments are given. Try to achieve four approval comments for every one disapproval, and watch the record for the evaluation. Sometimes parents practice being nice when no one is around.

Scientific Application

Example 51

Pinpoint: *Arson in home.*
                     (7-year-old boy)

Record: Boy setting fires for two years in home, always in presence of
                     matches and absence of parents (average one to two times
                     weekly).

Consequate: (1) Father informed son fire setting would result in loss of
                         highly-prized baseball mitt.
                     (2) Matches or match cover brought to parents received 5¢.
                         Matches "planted" around house for boy to find, although
                         told not to expect money every time.
                     (3) Boy bold he *could* strike full pack of matches under super-
                         vision, but for each match left unstruck he would receive 1¢
                         (first time earned 10¢, second time earned 17¢, third time
                         earned 20¢).
                     (4) Father gave verbal approval throughout program.

Evaluate: Boy brought all matches he could find to parents, stopped strik-
                     ing matches, ceased setting fires (entire instructional program
                     only four weeks long); no fire-setting instances eight months
                     later.

Note: Match seeking and bringing to parents as well as thinking one-
                     self "responsible" are incompatible with fire setting. The natural
                     "approval" for setting fires (brightness, excitement, etc.) was
                     made less desirable than the alternate approval from parents
                     (praise and money) and ultimately, self-approval. It is also
                     noted that parents taught boy when he could strike matches. The
                     procedure was helped by the threat of disapproval (loss of
                     glove).

Scientific Application

Example 52

Pinpoint:	*Disruptive behaviors during rest time in school.* (nineteen 6- to 7-year-old children)
Record:	Average inappropriate behavior was 54% (trained observers for ten days). Teacher gave praises or reprimands twelve times during ten- to fifteen-minute rest period.
Consequate:	Teacher contingently praised appropriate behavior, ignored disruptive behavior (twelve praise comments per day, only two reprimands in eight-day observation).
Evaluate:	Disruptive behavior averaged 32%.
Consequate II:	Teacher reprimanded so no one except disruptive child could hear (eleven per day—no praise seven days).
Evaluate II:	Disruptive behavior averaged 39%.
Consequate III:	Disapproval comments contingent on inappropriate behavior loud enough for entire class to hear (fourteen per day, no approval for five days).
Evaluate III:	Disruptive behavior increased to an average of 53%.
Consequate IV:	Teacher praised appropriate behavior, ignored inappropriate behavior (five days—twelve approval comments).
Evaluate IV:	Disruptive behavior averaged 35%.
Note:	In this scientific study the teacher controlled disruptive behavior by praising and reprimanding quietly. Loud reprimands (yelling?) increased rather than decreased the inappropriate behavior. A combination of approval for appropriate behavior and firm statements to the individual offender often serves to control young children very well. Quiet reprimands eliminate the possibility of the other children paying undue attention to the misbehaving child. Mothers may often resort to loud reprimands when a quiet firm statement may do more to increase appropriate behavior. This study with professional observers and changes in consequences to find the effect of changing intensity has direct home application.

Scientific Application

Example 53

Pinpoint: *Breaking household rules.*
(3- and 4-year-old boys)

Record: From 9 to 12 noon, mother's recording (six days) indicated an average of twenty-nine daily rule violations—playing in toilet, pulling dog's tail, climbing in kitchen, breakable items removed from cupboards, toys left out, changing TV and stereo knobs, taking telephone off hook, throwing artificial fruit; i.e., "doing the don'ts." Mother "caught the boys" about twenty-two times daily and (1) told them "why" what they were doing was wrong (reasoning), (2) scolded them, and (3) either slapped their hands or bottoms. Mother remarked, "Why can't they just play and stay out of things until I get the housework done; I play with them in the afternoons."

Consequate: Mother instructed to (1) ignore minor deviations unless someone could be hurt, (2) give great deal of praise for good behavior; that is, "catch each child being good" and verbally praise at least five times per hour each day, at same time pass out chips, let boys "spend" them later on "goodies," (3) use approval for one child when the other is inappropriate; for instance, "you're playing nicely, you didn't turn the TV dials, (after brother has turned dials), (4) when disapproval is warranted punish immediately with no talking or warning, generally by complete isolation, for a period of at least four minutes, and (5) go over household rules each morning plus three to four times per day when boys *are following* rules, *not* when they are disobedient.

Evaluate: Mother praised each child on an average of thirteen times per morning. She also stated other instructions were followed. Disapproval averaged thirty-four during first three days with twenty-seven isolations. Mother called consultant to report records and said behavior "hadn't changed" but had increased. Conversation indicated behavior change had indeed taken place (an increase in misbehavior). Mother instructed to maintain the contingencies for ten days. Next day (fourth) misbehavior decreased (twenty-three) with further daily decreases to average of three per day (ninth day).

Note: Disapproval (corporal punishment) was used in this case to stop inappropriate behavior as well as isolation. When removing the child from a positive surrounding, one must be certain that isolation is not more rewarding (e.g., playroom) than the closeness and verbal approval of the mother. Parents should also realize when starting new routines, as in this case, payoffs have been received for a long time by "doing the don'ts." Reasoning

General Observation Form

PINPOINT *Breaking rules*   Person(s) observed *Todd & Sam*
Observer(s) *Mother*   Location *Where playing*
Time of obs. *9:00–12:00*   Desire that behavior increase (decrease)

I (we) will conduct ___*1*___ observations per *day* every *day* for *6 days*
(number)   (min-hr-day)   (day-wk)   (day-wk)
before consequating takes place.

Observation interval ___*3 hours*___   Time between obs. *24 hours*
(sec-min-hr-day)   (sec-min-hr-day)

RECORD — Each occurrence of Pinpoint			CONSEQUATE — Consequences following occurrence of behavior					EVALUATE — Each occurrence of Pinpoint		
Date	Obs #		Date	Obs #	Approval	Dis-approval	Other	Date	Obs #	
5/12	1	卌 卌 卌	5/19	1	卌 卌 l	卌 卌 卌		6/2	1	llll
"	"	卌 卌 卌	"	"		卌 卌 卌		6/3	2	lll
"	"	卌 llll	"	"		卌 lll		6/4	3	l
5/13	2	卌 卌 卌	5/20	2	卌 卌 卌 l	卌 卌 卌		6/5	4	llll
"	"	卌 卌 卌	"	"		卌 卌 卌		6/6	5	—
"	"	llll	"	"		lll		6/7	6	l
5/14	3	卌 卌 卌	5/21	3	卌 卌 llll	卌 卌 卌				
"	"	卌 卌 l	"	"		卌 卌 卌 l				
5/15	4	卌 卌 卌	5/22	4	卌 卌 卌 l	卌 卌 卌				
"	"	卌 卌 卌	"	"		卌 lll				
"	"	lll	5/23	5	卌 卌 lll	卌 卌 卌				
5/16	5	卌 卌 卌	"	"		lll				
"	"	卌 lll	5/24	6	卌 卌 卌 l	卌 卌 lll				
5/18	6	卌 卌 卌	5/25	7	卌 卌 l	卌 lll				
"	"	卌 卌 lll	5/26	8	卌 ll	卌 卌				
			5/27	9	卌 卌 lll	lll				
			5/28	10	卌 卌 ll	lll				

Total = *183*   Totals = *29*   *80*   Total = *13*
# Obs. = *6*   # Obs. = *6*
Average = *29*   Average = *2+*

When *Todd & Sam cooperate*   When *Todd & Sam*
(appropriate)   (inappropriate)
for *5 times in hrs.*   Then this
(time-times)   disapproval
Then these approvals   will follow:
will follow: a. *isolation for 4 min-*
a. *praise*   *utes after*
b. *tokens*   *quiet*
c. *modeling*

Comments *5/17-just had to leave; 5/22 Isn't going to work; 5/23-they said to continue; 6/2-I like the morning again; 6/7-playing games with boys*

Summary:
Record total *183*
Evaluate total *13*
Record average *29*
Evaluate avg. *2+*
Increase _____
Decrease *26+*
per day

97

followed by spanking many times functions to increase the undesired behavior, especially when a parent is busy, and gives
attention generally only when the child misbehaves. Young
children learn very fast to get a mother's attention by misbehaving. Later when the payoff is removed children will try for long
periods to get attention in the way that has been rewarded in
the past. When the attention is not forthcoming, the child will
try even harder, i.e., increase the rate of inappropriate behavior,
until the new contingency is learned.

Professional Application

Example 54

Pinpoint:	*Neurodermatitis (scratching).* (22-year-old male)
Record:	Skin irritation (bleeding, itching) prevalent (two years); some-times, as often as twice a week, slept only two hours.
Consequate:	Electric shock administered by behavioral therapist in session wheneven scratching occurred. Relaxation techniques used to relieve frustration from urges to scratch.
Evaluate:	Six weeks of treatment stopped scratching; after nine weeks skin problem disappeared.
Note:	Parents often must decide whether or not to use strong dis-approval to stop some behaviors. When a strong disapproval is used there should be clearly defined alternate behaviors for the child. Should problems arise parents think extremely severe, professional help should be sought immediately. (Association for Advancement of Behavior Therapy would be pleased to sup-ply names of behaviorally oriented professionals in your locale.)

Scientific Application

Example 55

Pinpoint: *Fear in young children.*
                 (separate studies concerning 600 children, infants and school
                 age)

Record: Parents reported in interviews overt signs of fear exhibited
                 whenever children confronted fearful situations.

Consequate: Following procedures reported effective by parents: (1) *Incom-
                 patible response.* Feared object or situation gradually introduced
                 into child's presence while child engaged in pleasurable activ-
                 ity. (2) *Gradual approach.* Child led by degrees (over a number
                 of days) to come closer and closer to feared object or partici-
                 pate in feared activity. (3) *Modeling.* Feared activity or object
                 made readily accessible to child while other children partici-
                 pated enjoyably.

Evaluate: Incompatible responses, gradual approach, and modeling elimi-
                 nated about 85% of children's fears according to parents.

Note: The following procedures were *not* successful: disapproval, so-
                 cial ridicule, scolding, verbal appeals, punishment, forcing child
                 to participate, or changing the child's activity whenever he was
                 afraid. When any fearful situation is *forced* upon a child fear is
                 sometimes *increased.* (*See* Example 26.)

Scientific Application

Example 56

Pinpoint: *Annoying child/adult interactions with company present.*
                 (six children, ages 2 to 11)

Record: Children engaged in attention-seeking interaction with com-
                 pany to point of embarrassment for adults and frustration for
                 children. (Average of sixteen objectionable behaviors per hour
                 when company present.)

Consequate: "Children visiting time"—fifteen to twenty minutes assigned at
                 beginning of evening party. Full attention given to children dur-
                 ing this time (guests not desiring any child time asked to come

General Observation Form

PINPOINT *Show-offs; calling, dancing, jumping* Person(s) observed *Chet (3 yrs.)*

Observer(s) *Father* Location *Living room*

Time of obs. *When company present* Desire that behavior increase (decrease)

I (we) will conduct ___*1*___ observations per *hour* every *party* for *3 parties*
              (number)   (min-hr-day)   (day-wk)   (day-wk)

before consequating takes place.

Observation interval *60 minutes*   Time between obs. *variable*
       (sec-min-hr-day)   (sec-min-hr-day)

RECORD — Each occurrence of Pinpoint			CONSEQUATE — Consequences following occurrence of behavior					EVALUATE — Each occurrence of Pinpoint		
Date	Obs #		Date	Obs #	Approval	Dis-approval	Other OWN VISITING TIME	Date	Obs #	
12/22	1	卌 卌 卌 |||| 2/13	1	卌 卌 卌 卌		✓	2/13	1	—
12/27	2	卌 卌 ||| ||| 卌					
12/31	3	卌 卌 卌	3/20	2	卌 卌 卌 卌			✓	3/20	2	—
								4/28	3	—

Total = *48*	Totals = *49*		*2*	Total = *0*
# Obs. = *3*	When *Chet interacts with guests*	When _____		# Obs. = *3*
Average = *16*	(appropriate)	(inappropriate)		Average = *0*

Comments *Chet was excited with attention + left without a fuss. John + Sue really like kids. I learned a lot from watching them reward Chet.*

for *15 minutes*
(time-times)
Then these approvals will follow:
a. *words-praise*
b. *expressions*
c. *cocktails and hors d'oeuvres*

Then this disapproval will follow:
a. _____

Summary:
Record total ___*48*___
Evaluate total ___*0*___
Record average ___*16*___
Evaluate avg. ___*0*___
Increase _____
Decrease ___*16*___
per party

thirty minutes later). Child/guest interaction encouraged; *no* adult/adult interactions maintained. Children given special plate of hors d'oeuvres and "kiddy cocktails." At end of period children either put to bed or required to leave adults and establish individual play without any interruption.

Evaluate:
"Happy parties." Children began to look forward to their own time and company verbalized concerning "delightful children."

Note:
Various children's schedules can be made to fit the individual circumstances of each situation. The main idea is to structure separate times for children/adult interactions as opposed to non-structured situations in which children are unwittingly reinforced for their annoying attention-seeking behaviors, and company becomes annoyed.

Professional Application

Example 57

Pinpoint:
Screaming, yelling, fighting between siblings.
(two boys, 3 and 6 years old)

Record:
Boys fought whenever alone, damaged toys and furniture, older boy had recently broken neighbor's window. Observers (trained) watched when mother was not present (sixty to ninety minutes daily). Inappropriate behaviors (kicking, hitting, pushing, name-calling, throwing objects at each other) and cooperative behaviors (asking for something, requesting help, pleasant talking, playing close), combined, produced a cooperative behavior ratio of 46% (cooperative behavior divided by cooperative behavior plus inappropriate behavior). Six-year-old boy professionally diagnosed as "immature and brain-damaged" as he was hyperactive, aggressive, and destructive. Observations indicated mother paid attention only after high-intensity inappropriate responses.

Consequate:
Cooperative responses given approval by placing small candies in mouth and saying "good" every time a cooperative response occurred during *first two days*. Approval (things and words) given every second to fourth cooperative behavior next two days.

Mother's helper (professional) told boys they would receive approval if they asked for things saying please and thank you, answered questions, and played nicely together. Instructions repeated each day. On the fifth day a token check mark system plus instructions instituted. Both boys' names written on chalkboard in playroom. Checks earned for cooperative behaviors were removed for inappropriate behaviors. Checks exchanged for candy bars, bubble gum, caps, kites, comic books, puzzles, small toys (total cost $10.67). Boys' "price" paid for goodies was continually increased. Candies discontinued on twelfth day; a check system only for last four days.

Evaluate: Cooperative play averaged 85% (sixteen consequate days). Gradual rise in cooperative behavior prevailed (last day 100%) even though prices increased throughout program.

Consequate II: Check system removed for five days (observers recorded behavior but did not dispense approval).

Evaluate II: Cooperative behavior declined when no approval given (average 50%).

Consequate III: Check system reinstated with mother taking over management second day. Cooperative behavior increased but since some intense fighting occurred periodically, mother added disapproval contingency. When either child kicked, hit, pushed, name-called, or threw object mother placed boy in bathroom (interesting items removed, closed door, and left him) for five minutes (last three minutes had to be quiet time for boy to rejoin group). Isolation used once per day for each child during first three days, only once overall during last four. Mother also increased amount of checks necessary for approval rewards (raised prices). Children cooperated for three days before purchase possible. Mother also given help in knowing when to use contact and words in approving manner.

Evaluate III: Combination of procedures, administered by mother, resulted in cooperative play ratio of 90%. Experiment in effect for an hour and half during day, but as study concluded both parents practiced using behavioral principles throughout day. Teacher of older boy reported school behaviors improved.

Note: Authors of this scientific study reported parents had probably extinguished many behaviors of the older boy for lack of attention except for very high-intensity behaviors which received much verbal and physical attention (many spankings). Following study, parents started to change, i.e., they reported using more approval to initiate and maintain appropriate behavior and established token systems for some household chores. Authors reported parents surprised that a "brain-damaged" child could respond. It would appear that placing these kinds of labels on children solves few if any problems and may even generate feelings of futility within the parents rather than determination to do the best job possible. Some parents give the problem away (abdicate responsibility) because child is brain-damaged, retarded, autistic, neurotic, emotionally disturbed or any number of labels which may lead to resignation rather than a behavioral analysis of what is possible. *Every* child is "normal" in many ways, and *every* child is abnormal in others.

Scientific Application

Example 58

Pinpoint:	*Toothbrushing at summer camp.* (eight boys, 10 to 12 years old)
Record:	Two instances. One boy brushed once in the morning and another boy, once in the evening. All others, zero (four days).
Consequate:	All instructed, "Go and brush your teeth" on returning to cabin for rest hour following noon meal.
Evaluate:	Thirteen instances of brushing, six during rest hour, six during evening, one during morning (eight days).
Consequate II:	Swimming in lake made contingent upon brushing during rest hour.
Evaluate II:	Boys (100%) brushed during rest hour on sixteen days; all but one brushed for another four days. No one brushed in the evening, and one boy brushed in the morning on one day only (twenty-one day records).
Consequate III:	Lake dried up for four days and contingency for brushing was removed.
Evaluate III:	Brushing stopped completely when lake dry.

Scientific Application

Example 59

Pinpoint: *Fear of water.*
                   (11.5-month-old girl)

Record: No previous fear of water until one day girl slipped in the bath-
                   tub, began screaming, and removed from tub. During next few
                   days child's fear of water generalized to faucets, wading pools,
                   and any bathing.

Consequate: Treatment steps consisted of gradual approach: placing toys in
                   empty tub, placing girl on kitchen tables surrounding sinks,
                   washing at diaper-changing time at first in bathroom sink, then
                   in tub. Mother gave praise, body contact, and toys for successful
                   attempts.

Evaluate: By 12.75 months, fully recovered. At thirteen months child
                   initiated responses to water; joyfully played in backyard wading
                   pool. Follow-up studies at age eighteen months and also age
                   forty-two months indicated no fear of water.

Note: Approval received for small increments like touching water,
                   splashing in cup, or other tiny behaviors can be used. This
                   method (successive approximations) is effective in overcoming
                   fears of many different varieties.

Scientific Application

Example 60

Pinpoint: *Biting younger sibling.*
                   (3-year-old boy)

Record: Mother reported many instances averaging three to four over one
                   day.

Consequate: Mother severely reprimanded and slapped every time.

Evaluate: Biting increased.

Consequate II: Mother told child, "When you bite your mouth must be clean.
                   When you want to bite you may, but your mouth must be clean
                   so your sister doesn't get sick from the dirty germs. When you

want to bite come and tell Mother, and I will make sure your mouth is clean."

Evaluate II: Boy came to his mother once. Mother had boy rinse out own mouth with liquid dishwashing soap while she told him how nice as was to get his mouth clean. Biting eliminated.

Note: Disapproval (soap in mouth) followed the intention to bite. The child learned that such a thought was not rewarding even though he had his mother's permission. Thus, the "thought" of biting was followed immediately by rinsing his mouth with soap. Another parent reported (same age child) that she washed the mouth calmly with soap "to kill all the germs following the bite" with similar results.

Professional Application

Example 61

Pinpoint: *Nightmares.*
(11-year-old girl)

Record: Awake in middle of night two to three times per week screaming. Child went to parents' bedroom. Parents comforted and talked to child for approximately twenty to thirty minutes before taking her back to bed.

Consequate: Parents/child wrote down frightening dream(s). When relaxed and snacking around table parents role-played each portion of dream starting with least frightening scene. Whenever girl became even slightly upset parents stopped for treats, talked about pleasant things, gave affection. Girl repeated during play-acting "it was only a dream." Parents reinforced continually and drew parallels with TV movies while watching "scary" shows with girl. Girl was instructed to turn on lights when awakened from a dream and repeat over and over, "it's only a dream." Next morning parents rewarded girl for not coming into their bedroom.

Evaluate: Following eight role-playing and eight nighttime sessions only two nightmares occurred. Next three weeks, nightmare free; only one occurred four weeks later. Two-year follow-up indicated dreams did not return.

Note: Parents must beware of inadvertently rewarding nightmares by providing a great deal of attention and comfort. The first time, parents would be well-advised to calmly take the child back to bed and have the child describe the differences between dreams and reality in a joking, not a serious, manner.

Professional Application

Example 62

Pinpoint: *Rewarding creativity.*
                (12-year-old boy)

Record: No evidence of child attempting different alternatives to problem solutions (five forty-five minute play periods—materials provided by father).

Consequate: Child rewarded with money for successfully demonstrating divergent solutions to (1) word games, (2) puzzles, (3) erector set construction, (4) societal problems, and (5) uses of materials (i.e., How many things could we build with . . .).

Evaluate: Child demonstrated an increase in solutions and alternatives (two or three for each situation).

Note: Much has been said regarding creativity. If many alternatives as opposed to one are reinforced, then the child will learn to be creative (i.e., to restructure past experiences in new and meaningful ways). *Creative structuring* of contingencies will usually change many past *associations*. Reinforcing many *associations* will usually promote greater *creativity*.

Professional Application

General Observation Form

PINPOINT _Number of problem solutions_ Person(s) observed _Paul_

Observer(s) _Father_ Location _Paul's room_

Time of obs. _evening_ Desire that behavior (increase) decrease

I (we) will conduct ___1___ observations per _week_ every _week_ for _5 wks._
       (number)   (min-hr-day)   (day-wk)   (day-wk)
before consequating takes place.

Observation interval _45 minutes_ Time between obs. _7 days_
       (sec-min-hr-day)   (sec-min-hr-day)

RECORD Each occurrence of Pinpoint | | | **CONSEQUATE** Consequences following occurrence of behavior | | | | | **EVALUATE** Each occurrence of Pinpoint | |

Date	Obs #	PROBLEMS 1 2 3 4 5	Date	Obs #	Approval	Dis-approval	Other	Date	Obs #	PROBLEMS 1 2 3 4 5
6/18	1	I I I I I	7/28	1	✓✓			9/12	1	II III II I10 III
6/26	2	I I I I I	8/4	2	✓✓✓			9/20	2	III III I III II
7/4	3	II I II I I	8/13	3	✓✓✓✓			9/26	3	III III II III II
			"	"	✓✓					
7/12	4	II I I I I	8/20	4	✓✓✓✓			10/15	4	II III II III III
			"	"	✓✓✓✓✓					
7/19	5	I-I II I	8/23	5	✓✓✓✓			11/2	5	III III II II III
			"	"	✓✓✓✓					
			"	"	✓✓✓					
			8/30	6	✓✓✓✓					
			"	"	✓✓✓✓✓					
			"	"	✓					

Total = _27_ Totals = _48_ _____ _____ Total = _____
# Obs. = _5_ # Obs. = _____
Average = _5.4_ When _Paul gives_ When _____ Average = _____
for 5 problems _more solutions_

Comments _I can't_ (appropriate) (inappropriate) Summary:
understand how for _each past one_ Then this
a scientist's son (time-times) disapproval Record total ___27___
is content with one Then these approvals will follow: Evaluate total ___66___
answer. 8/23 - He's will follow: a. _____ Record average ___5.4___
getting the idea. a. _25¢_ Evaluate avg. ___13.2___
10/15 - Paul says he b. _____ Increase ___7.8___
enjoys looking. c. _____ Decrease _____

Example 63

Pinpoint:
Self-help behaviors.
(4.5-year-old boy)

Record:
Nothing. Boy born blind, severe hearing problem, could not walk, braces on legs, not toilet trained, said no words, could not feed self. (Tested I.Q. of 22.) Mother waiting to admit boy to large custodial hospital for mentally retarded.

Consequate:
Pediatrician assured mother that boy was in good health and that food deprivation would not be harmful for up to thirty-six hours; mother instructed to not use spoon but to place Rob in high chair, put his fingers in food and lift food to his mouth on his own fingers, three meals daily for two weeks. Following this procedure, his mother prepared Rob's favorite food, sat him in high chair, put his fingers in food, lifted them to within two inches of his mouth, then dropped her hand (this repeated until Rob fed himself or until it had been done 120 times at which time he was taken out of chair and not placed back for period of two hours).

Evaluate:
Rob cried when mother dropped her hands, threw his food, and made what mother called "his angry noises." Rob did not eat until deprived of food for thirty-four hours, and mother left house twice because of his "terrible crying and whimpering."

Note:
Most very young children have learned thousands of cause-and-effect relationships regarding consequences of their own behavior, but in this case this young boy had not learned even the very first (i.e., put food in mouth, swallow, pleasant sensation). He had only learned the latter part of the sequence with no causal relationship between *his* internal behavior and the behavior of the outside environment, i.e., getting food into his mouth. Starvation was used to maximize the effect of pleasure derived from the food. This boy, through elaborate series of shaping procedures, learned how to find his own way around the house (rolling to his food from ever greater distances as he couldn't walk), toilet training (using liquid juice as a reward), verbalizations (pairing feel and words starting with body parts), play skills (through the use of contingent music), and then progressed to more normal activities of childhood. These procedures allowed this child first to be placed in a private school for the retarded (behaviorally oriented) and later to enroll in a normal kindergarten. After three years follow-up the child has progressed normally into and through the public schools. Extremely strong contingencies were necessary in this program which started *where the boy was*. It sometimes must be remembered that there is an infinite distance between zero and one.

Professional Application

General Observation Form

PINPOINT *Feeding self* Person(s) observed *Rob*

Observer(s) *Mother* Location *Kitchen*

Time of obs. *meals* Desire that behavior (increase) decrease

I (we) will conduct __3__ observations per *day* every *day* for *4 days*
 (number) (min-hr-day) (day-wk) (day-wk)

before consequating takes place.

Observation interval *30 minutes* Time between obs. *between meals*
 (sec-min-hr-day) (sec-min-hr-day)

RECORD Each occurrence of Pinpoint			CONSEQUATE Consequences following occurrence of behavior					EVALUATE Each occurrence of Pinpoint		
Date	Obs #		Date	Obs #	Approval	Dis-approval	Other	Date	Obs #	
9/3	1	—	9/7		*helped*			10/1	1	卌 卌 卌 卌 .
	2	—	to		*every meal*					卌 卌 卌 卌
	3	—	9/20		*every day*				2	卌 卌 卌 卌
9/4	1	—								卌 卌 卌 卌 I
	2	—	9/21	1	—				3	卌 卌 卌
	3	—		2	—					卌 卌 卌
9/5	1	—		3	—					卌 卌 III
	2	—	9/22	1	—			10/2	1	卌 卌 卌 卌
	3	—		2	—					卌 卌 卌 卌
9/6	1	—		3	—				2	卌 卌 卌 卌
	2	—	9/23	1	卌 卌 卌 III					卌 卌 III
	3	—		2	卌 卌 III				3	卌 卌 卌 卌
				3	卌 卌 卌 10					卌 卌 卌 II
								10/3	1	卌 卌 卌 卌
										卌 卌 卌 I
									2	卌 卌 卌 卌
										卌 卌 I
									3	卌 卌 卌 卌
										卌 III

Total = __0__ Totals = __51__ Total = __329__
\# Obs. = __12__ \# Obs. = __9__
Average = __0__ Average = __37.7__

When *Rob puts food in mouth* (appropriate) for *anything* (time-times) Then these approvals will follow:
a. *candy*
b. *praise*
c. *kiss & love*

When *Rob cries* (inappropriate) Then this disapproval will follow:
a. *remove plate for short time*

Comments *Help put food in mouth for 2 weeks. 9/21- The crying is terrible. Had to call. 9/22- He ate today. 10/3- He can start with spoon.*

Summary:
Record total __0__
Evaluate total __329__
Record average __0__
Evaluate avg. __37?__
Increase __37__
Decrease __per meal__

109

Example 64

Pinpoint: *Homework study*
(17-year-old girl in high school)

Record: Grades monitored for one semester. Average grade D, with frequent failures.

Consequate: Flash cards developed by student to assist study in history, civics, Latin. Meals contingent (except breakfast) upon success in responses to cards.

Evaluate: Within eight weeks grades rose from D to a B average.

Note: Researchers noted the flash cards may have been reinforcing instead of the food. However, a follow-up at a later semester indicated grades had returned to a D average. Obviously, cards or grades alone were not sufficient rewards for this girl. Motivation must come from without before it gets "in." The question of how long it takes for motivation to "get in" for each individual is not known. However, it would appear that even constant rewarding is better than constant failure.

Scientific Application

Example 65

Pinpoint: *Requesting privilege from one parent after being turned down by other parent.*
(preschoolers)

Record: Four instances one week.

Consequate: Parent overheard one child request sister to ask his mother for a joint play privilege previously denied by the father. Parent "shamed" child for being "sneaking" (children's own word for dishonest) until soft crying appeared. Child sent from room. Following thirty minutes isolation father recalled girl, happily stated, "We are going to learn how to be honest and *not* sneaky." Father asked child, "Machelle, if Daddy says you cannot go out to swing, should you ask Mother?" Child given increasingly more difficult verbal and role-playing tasks to discriminate honest from dishonest behavior, with father applying rules to familial interactions. "If Mother says she is too busy to do something, is it all right to ask Daddy?" Later tasks included approval for honesty in reporting discrepancies, i.e., one parent tells child it is right for her to do something after other parent, outside of earshot, has previously given prohibition. "Show me what you would do if Mother told you one thing and Daddy told you another."

Evaluate: No more incidences of asking other parent. Later child also very careful in always reporting directions given by other parent.

Professional Application

Example 66

Pinpoint: *Aggression: hitting and disapproving verbal comments.* (twenty-seven 3- and 4-year-old boys in nursery school)

Record: Physical aggression frequency totaled 41.2; verbal aggression, 22.8—with total of 64.0 (one-week observation).

Consequate: Teachers ignored aggression and rewarded cooperative and peaceful behaviors (interfered only when bodily harm was likely). Approval techniques replaced reprimands.

Evaluate: Total aggressive behaviors decreased—64 to 43.4. (Physical aggression, 41.2 to 26.0; verbal aggression, 22.8 to 17.4.)

Consequate II: Following initial consequate, researchers told that teachers' experiment was completed; however, observations again recorded three weeks later.

Evaluate II: After experimenter left, teachers not as consistent. Total number aggressive responses increased 43.4 to 51.6. Physical aggression increased 26.0 to 37.8. However, verbal aggression decreased 16.4 to 13.8. (Teachers, as well as most parents, find it harder to ignore fighting than to ignore verbal threats.)

Consequate III: Consequate I reinstated.

Evaluate III: Total aggression decreased 51.6 to 25.6. Physical aggression decreased 37.8 to 21.0; verbal aggression, 13.8 to 4.6.

Note: This study substantiates the necessity of *absolute consistency*. Adults must follow through if behavioral change is to be maintained.

Scientific Application

Example 67

Pinpoint: *Cigarette smoking.*
                     (five male and three female college students)

Record: Smoking rate was between one and one and a half packs per day (average time since beginning smoking was 2.6 years).

Consequate: All subjects instructed to smoke four packs per day.

Evaluate: Six persons quit and did not resume smoking. One person did not participate; one resumed two days after quitting.

Note: Many behavioral methods have been used to help people stop smoking. While most parents are aware of their children's smoking shortly after child begins, even after an average of 2.6 years, most of the college students quit with the satiation technique. This represents nothing more than what Grandpa did when he made his son finish a whole box of cigars after hearing he had smoked one. There is one added benefit when the young person has not yet acquired the habit. Excessive smoking, perhaps even more than in this experiment, will often induce nausea which may become associated with the urge of smoke. It is recommended that parents should not be punitive; merely sit down with the youngster and insist pack after pack of cigarettes are smoked with inhaling every ten to twenty seconds. This procedure does not insure that smoking will not resume, but seems better than most other techniques for teen-agers who have a hard time looking toward the end of a term in high school let alone being motivated by the fear of disease forty years away.

Scientific Application

Example 68

Pinpoint: *Crying when parents leave.*
                    (eighteen children, infants through 6 years old)

Record: Parents recorded children crying and clinging an average of nine to twelve times and also commented on "general upsetness" when parents ready to leave child with sitter (fifteen minutes prior to leaving, two to six observations).

Consequate: Parents "proved" to child they always come back (building hope in the child). Parents kissed child goodbye, ignored clinging, left immediately, walked around house, came back in the door. (Parents instructed to always wait until crying ceased before reentering.) Parents again left following same routine (hug and kiss), promising to return shortly. (Any hesitation at door reinforces crying; it is even worse to comfort child after he begins to cry, which teaches him that if he is upset enough he can delay parents exit.) This same procedure followed for varying lengths of time (ten seconds, two minutes, thirty seconds, four minutes, one minute, six minutes, etc., the technique is then expanded to longer periods of time.) About every third time a special little treat is given to the child for being nice when parents arrive.

Evaluate: Goodbyes became happy times as children anticipate parents sometimes coming back with special small toys or treats.

Note: It is suggested to parents that when they begin this program for the first time, they begin at least two hours prior to normal departure time.

Professional Application

Example 69

Pinpoint: *Fear of school presentations.*
                    (four 6th grade girls, social studies class)

Record: Number of times girls volunteered during two-week period: zero. Only six questions answered when specifically directed toward them. Girls not chosen by classmates for play or committee work.

General Observation Form

PINPOINT *Crying and clinging* Person(s) observed *Cindy*
Observer(s) *Parents and sitter* Location *Front door*
Time of obs. *15 min. before leaving* Desire that behavior increase (decrease)
until 15 min. after

I (we) will conduct _____/_____ observations per *leaving*
(number) *day* every *time* for *5 times*
(min-hr-day) (day-wk) (day-wk)

before consequating takes place.

Observation interval *30 minutes* Time between obs. *unknown*
(sec-min-hr-day) (sec-min-hr-day)

RECORD — Each occurrence of Pinpoint			CONSEQUATE — Consequences following occurrence of behavior					EVALUATE — Each occurrence of Pinpoint		
Date	Obs #		Date	Obs #	Approval	Dis-approval	Other	Date	Obs #	
Sun.	1	ℳℳℳ	Sat.	1	ℳℳ			Sat.	1	1
Fri.	2	ℳ ////	Wed.	2	ℳ //			Fri.	2	//
Sat.	3	ℳ ////	Sun.	3	ℳ /			Sun.	3	—
Fri.	4	ℳ ℳ ℳ/	Fri.	4	////			Fri.	4	—
Sun	5	ℳ ℳ //	Sat.	5	/ (in a hurry)			Sat.	5	—
			Wed.	6	////					
			Fri.	7	///					
			Wed.	8	//					

Total = **61** Totals = **37** _____ _____ Total = **3**
# Obs. = **5** # Obs. = **5**
Average = **12.2** When *Cindy plays when we go* When _____ Average = **0.6**
(appropriate) (inappropriate)

Comments *I don't think this will work. She needs my love and my husband doesn't understand. Evaluate—Cindy is a pleasure for the sitter now.*

for *variable*
(time-times)
Then these approvals will follow:
a. *words-spoken*
b. *hugging, kissing*
c. *things, prizes*

Then this disapproval will follow:
a. _____

Summary:
Record total _____ **61**
Evaluate total _____ **3**
Record average _____ **12.2**
Evaluate avg. _____ **0.6**
Increase _____
Decrease _____ **11.4**
per time

Consequate: Activities developed with approval from teacher and classmates. Girls recited alone from assigned book, read passages for parents—who praised accomplishment—then read for teacher alone. Girls' voices recorded and positive verbal approval given by teacher for effective talking. Recording later played for entire class, which praised performance. Teacher also praised interaction with other children. Additionally, small groups of girls worked on projects. Each group started with one fearful girl and one girl who modeled appropriate behavior; number of students gradually increased.

Evaluate: Volunteering in class increased from nothing to an average slightly below rest of class.

Note: These procedures are closely related to many learning situations where initial fear is gradually reduced by participating in the fear-producing activity (or approaching the feared objects) in small steps, receiving approval for behavior which is incompatible with avoidance.

Professional Application

Example 70

Pinpoint: *Excessive handkerchief clutching.*
(college age girl)

Record: Sinus trouble, recorded clutching handkerchief 90% of all waking time.

Consequate: Discriminations between holding handkerchief when needed/not needed. Handkerchief not allowed during on-task study time, following sinus pill, when nose dry, during eating time, etc. Also, girl changed to tissues, required herself to recite following jingle prior to using:

> Blow your nose,
> Wipe it clean;
> Then place the rag
> So it can't be seen.

Girl instructed friends and boyfriend to remind her when handkerchief was out.

Evaluate: Seven weeks later handkerchief holding reduced to 20% of re-
                   corded time.

Note: The girl reported in this self-directed routine that discrimina-
                   tions between when to hold and when not to hold her handker-
                   chief were developed. Contingencies employed served basically
                   as reminders (cues) which helped her to keep handkerchief out
                   of sight.

Professional Application

Example 71

Pinpoint: *Lawbreaking.*
                   [forty 17.8-year-old (average) delinquent boys]

Record: Average age at first arrest 13.5; average number of arrests 8.2;
                   total time incarcerated 15.1 months. All boys arrested approxi-
                   mately same age, same nationality, equal number of months in
                   jail, similar residence and religious preferences.

Consequate: One group participated in consequences while "control" group
                   did not. Boys not in school (most of them should have been)
                   were met on street corners or other places of frequent occu-
                   pancy. Each boy offered job and told researcher wanted to know
                   "how teen-agers felt about things." Boys who participated re-
                   warded with food, cokes, money, or tokens, depending upon each
                   individual case. No punishment employed. Occasionally, bonus
                   rewards given for prompt arrival, proper verbalizations, and
                   spontaneous interest.

Evaluate: Groups compared three years later. Consequate group averaged
                   2.4 arrests, other group 4.7; average number of months in jail
                   3.5 for consequate group, 6.9 for other group. Illegal acts com-
                   mitted by consequate group less frequent and much less severe.

Note: In this particular study, consequences were not directed toward
                   criminal behavior itself but represented an attempt to teach pro-
                   social behavioral patterns. When a boy did not appear, the re-
                   searcher would meet him out on the street and bring him to the
                   lab. It is sometimes important to go after a child and bring him

where he should be. Any peer group such as the above juvenile group can exercise tremendous pressure toward group conformity. Often peer rewards must be broken down or changed if the parent is to succeed.

Scientific Application

Example 72

Pinpoint: *"Inappropriate" sexual advances.*
         (16-year-old girl)

Record: Six cases of boys responding on dates with sexually aggressive behavior opposite to that desired by girl (last school term, following recent move to new school).

Consequate: Girl instructed (practiced role-playing with father) in delivering verbal response and changing bodily responses in order to elicit more "appropriate," less "inappropriate," responses from male peers. Girl instructed to dress differently.

Evaluate: "Inappropriate" sexual behavior decreased to zero after four weeks. Dating also decreased by one-half.

Note: This girl, like many others, was making the mistake of "selling tomatoes" when, in fact, she was really "lettuce." Effective social behavior is made up of correctly interpreting and giving cues. If a person wants to have "lettuce" bought, this is what one should sell. If one determines (as in above case) that more "tomatoes" are being purchased and wants to entice the buyer into the store, then one should be prepared for the consequences. Regardless, parents should not be naive in assessing the effects of their own actions. The mother of the girl in the above case was "furious with the way boys viewed her daughter" in clothes the mother had purchased.

Professional Application

General Observation Form

PINPOINT *Sexual advances*   Person(s) observed *Donna*

Observer(s) *Donna—Father for role-playing* Location *On dates*

Time of obs. *On date*   Desire that behavior increase (decrease)

I (we) will conduct __*1*__ observations per __*date*__ every __*date*__ for __*10 dates*__
(number)   (min-hr-day)   (day-wk)   (day-wk)

before consequating takes place.

Observation interval __*evening*__   Time between obs. __*unknown*__
(sec-min-hr-day)   (sec-min-hr-day)

RECORD Each occurrence of Pinpoint			CONSEQUATE Consequences following occurrence of behavior					EVALUATE Each occurrence of Pinpoint		
Date	Obs #		Date	Obs #	Approval	Dis-approval	Other	Date	Obs #	
Joe	1	III	M-Fri.	1	✓✓✓✓	✓	dress	Frank	1	1
Frank	2	ⅦⅠ III						Bill	2	—
Harold	3	II	M-Fri.	2	✓✓✓✓			Sam	3	1
Bill	4	—						Bill	4	—
Dan	5	III	M-Fri.	3	✓✓✓✓			Harold	5	II
Bill	6	—						Bill	6	—
Joe	7	IIII	M-Fri.	4	✓✓✓✓	✓	dress	Dan	7	1
Bill	8	—						Bill	8	—
Sam	9	ⅦⅠ III						Frank	9	—
Bill	10	—						Frank	10	—

Total = *28*   Totals = *20*   *2*   Total = *5*

\# Obs. = *10*   # Obs. = *10*

Average = *2.8*   When *Donna role-plays*   When *Donna dresses sexy*   Average = *0.5*

(appropriate)   (inappropriate)   Summary:

Comments _____   for *non-sexual actions*   Record total ____ *28*

_____   (time-times)   Then this   Evaluate total ____ *5*

_____   Then these approvals   disapproval   Record average ____ *2.8*

_____   will follow: will follow: Evaluate avg. ____ *0.5*

_____   a. *praise*   a. *father's reprimand & explanation*   Increase ____

_____   b. _____   Decrease ____ *2.3*

_____   c. _____   *per date*

118

Example 73

Pinpoint: *Discrimination "courage" behavior.*
                  (8-year-old boy)

Record: Boy home later from school after beating by "bully." Boy told
                  his mother he didn't want to tell his father because he was a
                  coward (one occurrence).

Consequate: Boy instructed in discriminating among fear, cowardism, cour-
                  age. Boy told that: (1) fear is perfectly okay in some situa-
                  tions, given some examples, (2) cowardism is when one does not
                  do what one thinks is right, again given examples, (3) courage
                  is the ability to deal with big things (such as some of the prob-
                  lems the boy was trying to overcome at school).

Evaluate: Boy did not fight, yet maintained strong "self-concept," i.e.,
                  self-report to father "I'm very afraid of that big fifth grader,
                  but I know it's his problem not mine."

Note: Many modern parents are ambivalent concerning fighting. While
                  some believe the child should fight, others believe that the child
                  should never fight, and most believe the child should not start a
                  fight yet should retaliate if put upon. Regardless of parental
                  views, it seems much more important as far as the child is
                  concerned that whatever the child does concerning fighting, he
                  should still have a good "self-concept" regarding his behavior.
                  Parents can accomplish this by "labeling" for the child and then
                  reinforcing whatever behavior they feel appropriate. However,
                  consistency *must* be maintained.

Professional Application

Example 74

Pinpoint: *Completion of household tasks.*
                  (8-, 11-, and 14-year-old brothers)

Record: *Off task* while working on assigned household tasks. Tasks not
                  completed during assigned times, "horseplay" between boys
                  whenever working closely together. Work not completed satis-
                  factorily for five straight days (checked by parents).

General Observation Form

PINPOINT *Chores completed* Person(s) observed *Dave, Joe, Fred*
Observer(s) *Father and mother* Location *Where assigned*
Time of obs. *Before supper* Desire that behavior (increase) decrease

I (we) will conduct ___*1*___ observations per *day* every *day* for *5 days*
   (number) (min-hr-day) (day-wk) (day-wk)
before consequating takes place.

Observation interval *10 minutes* Time between obs. *24 hours*
   (sec-min-hr-day) (sec-min-hr-day)

RECORD Each occurrence of Pinpoint			CONSEQUATE Consequences following occurrence of behavior					EVALUATE Each occurrence of Pinpoint		
Date	Obs #	D J F	Date	Obs #	Approval *supper*	Dis-approval	Other	Date	Obs #	D J F
Mon.	1	– – –	Sat.	1				Mon.	1	IIII III II
			Dave			✓				
Tues.	2	– – –	Joe			✓		Tues.	2	IIII III II
			Fred		✓					
Wed.	3	1 – –	Mon.	2				Wed.	3	IIII III II
			Dave			✓				
Thurs.	4	– – 1	Joe		✓			Thurs.	4	IIII III II
			Fred		✓					
Fri.	5	1 – –	Tues.	3				Fri.	5	IIII III II
			Dave			✓				
			Joe		✓					
			Fred			✓				
			Wed.	4						
			Dave			✓				
			Joe		✓					
			Fred		✓					
			Thurs.	5						
			Dave		✓					
			Joe		✓					
			Fred		✓					

Total = *3*   Totals = *9*   *6*   Total = *45*
# Obs. = *5*   # Obs. = *5*
Average = *0.6*   Average = *9*

When *boys complete work* (appropriate)   When *boys do not do chores* (inappropriate)
for *each day* (time-times)   Then this disapproval will follow:
Then these approvals will follow: a. *no supper*
a. *supper*
b. _____
c. _____

Comments *Dave seems too old. I wonder if we are making a mistake. He finally came around. He's stubborn like his dad.*

Summary:
Record total ___*2*
Evaluate total ___*45*
Record average ___*0.4*
Evaluate avg. ___*9.0*
Increase ___*8.6*
Decrease ___*per day*

Consequate: Children and parents decided together that mealtime in eve-
               nings is contingent on work tasks completed to parent's satis-
               faction. Parent checked assignment just prior to evening meal. If
               tasks complete, plate on the table. It task either not completed
               or did not meet with approval, *no* plate on dinner table; boy
               calmly denied privilege of supper.

Evaluate: Tasks all completed to satisfaction after total of six meals
               missed—four by fourteen year old.

Note: Parents were able to let the situation do the punishing and be-
               come "benevolent disapprovers." Once contingencies are struc-
               tured the parents can be very sorry that the child does not get
               supper: "I'm sorry you didn't get your work done, now you
               don't get to eat your supper; but, it was your responsibility."
               The child is unable to give the problem to the parent—as many
               times occurs when the parent gets angry or is the physical pun-
               isher or screamer. Thus the child learns to take responsibility for
               his own actions. In the above example the fourteen-year-old
               boy decided that he didn't like the contingencies, after, not
               before, missing one meal and decided not to do any work. This
               lasted for four days with no special comments from his parents.
               (Later the mother confessed that when he was hungry she really
               wanted to fix a snack for him, late at night.) Had she suc-
               cumbed the boy would have learned just what he was taught;
               that is, if you don't do your work and suffer awhile, then you'll
               finally be rewarded.

Professional Application

Example 75

Pinpoint: *"Disobedience" and "aggression."*
               (4-year 8-month-old boy)

Record: Trained observers recorded occurrence or nonoccurrence one
               hour per day (percent of time intervals behavior occurred).
               Aggression—defined as hitting, pushing, kicking, throwing, bit-
               ing, and scratching—occurred 7.7% of the time and disobedi-
               ence—defined as not following instructions by mother which
               included name and a command to do or stop doing something

specific—occurred 70.0% of the time (average for ten-day observation period). Observers noted that mother gave approval to undesirable behavior and was inconsistent in techniques of reinforcement.

Consequate: Appropriate behavior received praise and "goodies." Whenever mother noted aggressive or disobedient behavior she would tell boy, "You may not stay here (yard or playroom, etc.) if you do not do as you are told," and rapidly take him to time-out (isolation) room and leave him for two minutes. All items of child interest had been removed from the room. Boy remained two minutes *after* he stopped crying, screaming, noise-making.

Evaluate: Aggression decreased to 1.2% and disobedience decreased to 22.0% (average for ten days of consequences with generally better behavior each day).

Consequate II: Mother returned to original routines, refrained from using "time-out" room.

Evaluate II: Aggression increased to 4.0%, disobedience increased to 57% (average for six days, however, disobedience was 80% on last day).

Consequate III: Mother used "time-out" (isolation) room and comments again as well as praise and "goodies" for appropriate obedience.

Evaluate III: Aggression decreased to 0.3% and disobedience to 22% (four days).

Note: Consistency in following a routine until behavior is changed is demonstrated by the mother applying consequences, removing consequences, and applying them again (reversals). Some children may take an extended period of time to "change wrong associations" and even longer to become "self-motivated." Any new program should have as much consistency as possible for two weeks before something new is attempted.

Scientific Application

Example 76

Pinpoint:	*Work-work tasks.* (8-, 12-, 14-year-old boys and girls)
Record:	Household chores assigned not completed without constant reminders—nagging (thirty-one instances in three days).
Consequate:	Two appropriate but difficult jobs assigned each day by parent in writing to each child. Records kept entirely by children. Money paid for presenting completed weekly records (on Saturday afternoons) showing fourteen jobs completed (various amount for each age level). Children responsible for records; if jobs not complete or not recorded correctly, no pay forthcoming. Payment given for complete, not partial, record.
Evaluate:	Recording errors noted first week (none later), although all assigned jobs completed on each day of program. Negative interaction between parents and children regarding work almost entirely eliminated.
Note:	Work-work tasks have never been easy for anyone to learn. Most parents think children should develop the ability to do what has to be done even if children don't "want to." Therefore, parents generally persist in exhortation, naggings, and punishments for lack of work. The above example used a positive method, let the situation do the punishing, and, more important, placed responsibility on the worker. An effective technique used when children first go out to work for others is to have them do the job *plus* one extra. Thus, after mowing the lawn, one might trim the hedges; while baby sitting, one might wash a few dishes. Usually this stimulates much positive reinforcement from the initial employer and thus increases the probability of further successes regarding work-work.

Professional Application

Example 77

Pinpoint: *Toilet training techniques: a comparison.*
                (seventy children ranging in age from 12 through 36 months)

Record: All mothers kept a one-week record of number of successful
                eliminations in the proper place, as well as number of accidents
                (mothers checked diapers every waking hour).

Consequate: Children were divided into five separate groups using different
                consequences over a four-week period.

                (a) *Maturational control group* of fifteen children. Parents were
                    instructed to do no training and wait for four weeks.
                (b) *Parents' methods group* of thirteen children recorded their
                    methods and trained in their own way for four weeks.
                (c) *Buzzer pants group* of fourteen children. Mothers provided
                    with miniature transistorized speaker (cigarette pack size)
                    which sounded when pants were wet.
                (d) *Reinforcement schedule plus buzzer pants group.* Mothers
                    used buzzer pants on child and also rewarded child's ap-
                    propriate approach and elimination.
                (e) *Reinforcement schedule group.* Mothers used reinforcement
                    schedule only.

Evaluate:

Groups	Successes Increases	Accidents Decreases
(a) Growing older	0.6	4.2
(b) Parents' methods	5.6	2.4
(c) Buzzer pants	5.1	15.0
(d) Reinforcement plus buzzer pants	19.1	23.6
(e) Reinforcement only	14.7	16.0

Note: It should be noted that the buzzer pants were effective in de-
                creasing accidents (remember that wetness caused the buzzer
                to sound) but were not very effective in increasing successes.
                Actually, toilet training is made up of *two* separate behaviors:
                appropriate elimination in the toilet as well as ability to inhibit
                inappropriate elimination elsewhere. Parents should reward ap-
                propriate toilet behavior and disapprove or ignore inappropriate
                responses. Also, the above study demonstrated that effective
                training may begin as early as sixteen months.

Since buzzer pants are normally unavailable or perhaps not desired by some
parents, the complete instructions to parents within the reinforcement group follow:

Equipment needed:
Toilet ("potty") chair. Restraints such as trays, straps, or toys
should be removed.

The chair should be the type that can both be used alone on the floor or placed on the toilet. (Casco or similar brand is excellent.) During the training period the potty chair should always be used on the floor of the bathroom.

Ample supply of child's favorite candy or treats (marshmallows, sweet cereals, mints, or other candies). The treat used *must* be one which is quickly consumed (no caramels or suckers). The treats may be kept in the bathroom out of the child's reach or, if you prefer, you may bring a treat to the child each time. Because of incorrect associations, we suggest that you do *not* keep the treats in the medicine cabinet.

General rules:

Please do *not deviate* from the schedule or the instructions at any time during the training phase.

Reward you child's eliminating in the appropriate place (potty chair) within *two seconds* after the process of elimination has begun. Also reward your child with treats and praise if he (she) tells you beforehand that he (she) has to go to the bathroom. This is the goal of the training procedure. For learning to take place in a very young child (one without many verbal skills) the *timing* of the reward is very important. Treats (when given on the toilet) should be given *before* the child stands up, washes his (her) hands, etc. Recognizing that cleanliness training is also important and to help you shorten the time between the *beginning* of elimination and the time your child eats the treat, place the treat directly in the child's mouth yourself. This should be done (treat in mouth) every time it is indicated on the training schedule. *Never* act or look disappointed when the child has an accident or refuses to come with you to the bathroom (facial disapproval). Never punish verbally or reprimand the child for either accidents or refusals. When these accidents occur (and they will) maintain a neutral and matter of fact attitude. Make sure, however, that you do *not* give any treats, smiles, attention, or praise when these accidents occur.

In order to maximize the value of the treats do *not* give the child the same or similar treats at any other time during the day or night. The treats should be something special (a reward for especially pleasing Mommy or Daddy). The natural bodily processes and toilet training in general will thus become positive rather than negative.

Your child's liquid intake should not be reduced when training. Have water or other liquids available at all times, including just before naps or bed. The training procedure will build the ability to retain liquids over longer periods of time.

The words you use to designate the toilet and the processes of elimination are completely up to you. We suggest using the natural terms (urination and defecation), but any words are acceptable as long as you are comfortable using them. Some children have no words for the elimination processes, and it may be necessary to train your child to use a particular word until it becomes interpretable by you.

Toilet training schedule—general instructions:

Progress should be recorded by the mother, father, or other responsible adult, such as a babysitter. Record each time the child is taken to the bathroom, the amount of time he (she) sits on the potty chair, mark whether urination and/or defecation occurs, the number of accidents during training, and the number of times the child asks you to take him (her) to the bathroom before any elimination has occurred. For record purposes, an accident is defined as any time the child urinates or defecates without telling the parent first. Should your child tell you after elimination has occurred, please note the occurrence on the record form but still count it as an accident.

Boys should sit down for initial training. We have found that it is quite simple to teach a boy to urinate standing up after he has mastered control rather than attempting to introduce an added problem at first.

It is important that the child eliminate as soon as possible in the "potty" chair. The sooner this is accomplished, the better; therefore, extra time spent in entertaining the child during the first few days of training will probably pay off in more efficient training. It is important to remember that the child should *never* be forced to stay on the toilet (no restraints on the potty chair). It is permissible to give more frequent treats during the early days of the program until elimination occurs four or five times in the appropriate place. Always give lavish praise when the child comes to you and indicates that he (she) has to go to the bathroom. When these forewarnings are followed by successful elimination in the potty chair, treats and additional praise should be given.

When training starts the child should *never* be left alone in the bathroom (and remember to use the potty chair on the floor only; do not put the potty on the toilet). The safety reasons for this are obvious. Additionally, the parent must be available to immediately deliver the reward for successful performance of the training tasks. If the mother comes into the room even moments after a child has eliminated and then praises him (her), there is no connection in the child's mind between the act and the praise (children cannot abstract like adults).

When the child properly eliminates while seated on the potty chair, the treat should be given within two seconds and the parent should be lavish with praise [for example, "Oh, that's wonderful," "What a big boy (girl) you are," "That makes Mommy happy," etc.] You may also give approval expressions such as hugs and kisses in addition to the praise and treats. The parent should then repeat the phrase, "When you _____ (use your own word here) in the potty, it makes Mommy happy and you get (name of treat)." Remember, your child is young and although you may think he (she) understands, it is necessary to repeat the phrase several times on each occasion. This same procedure should be followed regardless of whether you are bringing the child to the bathroom because it is indicated in the schedule or because the child asks you first.

It is very important to spend as much time as possible playing with or entertaining your child while he (she) sits on the potty. Patience and a relatively small investment of time early in the training sequence will pay large dividends later on. As long as the child makes no attempt to get up and is enjoying the games, toys, or stories, he (she) can remain on the potty (but do not exceed twelve minutes at any one time). When the child wants to get up, let him (her) up, as nothing negative should be connected with the training procedure.

When the child comes to you and indicates in some way that he (she) has to go to the bathroom, tell the child that, "It makes Mommy very happy when you tell her that you have to go to the bathroom." Then place the child on the potty chair and tell him (her): "When you _____ in the potty, it makes Mommy happy and you get _____." If the child successfully eliminates while on the potty, give treats and praise.

First training week:

When your child comes to you and asks to go to the toilet, he (she) should be taken but the treat should be given only when he (she) gets up (after elimination or meeting the minimum time requirement) not when he (she) sits down. When you take the child during this week reward both sitting down and meeting the minimum time and/or elimination.

Day 1:

Take your child into the bathroom, show him (her) the candy and say "When you sit on the potty you get candy." Set the child on the toilet and give him (her) the candy treat. Follow the same procedure on a regular schedule of four times per day: (1) one hour after getting up or just before breakfast; (2) just before lunch, (3) one hour after nap, (4) right before evening dinner. You should also take your child to the bathroom an additional two times per day and follow the same general procedure, i.e., say, "When you _____ in the potty it makes Mommy happy and you get _____ (name of treat)." You can also say, "When you have to _____ in the potty tell Mommy. When you _____ in the potty it makes Mommy happy and you get _____ (your treat)." Reward with a treat if the child indicates he (she) should go to the bathroom or goes by himself (herself).

This early period is to familiarize the child with the bathroom and the potty chair. Even if you feel that your child is already familiar with the bathroom and the potty, please follow through on this phase of the schedule nonetheless.

The child should stay on the potty chair for at least two minutes if possible; however, allow the child to get up if he (she) desires even after only a few seconds. If elimination does not occur, he (she) should be given another treat while the parent repeats the "When you go in the potty . . ." If the child succeeds in urinating or defecating while seated on the potty chair, praise him (her) and give an additional treat and praise. Whenever the child receives treats and praise for going in the potty chair, say: "Come and tell Mommy when you have to _____ ."

You may play with or otherwise entertain your child for up to twelve minutes this first day during the regularly scheduled trips to the potty. Your child should be allowed to get up when he (she) desires and no restraints (trays or straps) should hold him (her) in the chair. Tell him (her) "When you _____ in the potty it makes Mommy happy and you get _____ (name of treat)."

Day 2:

Same as day 1 except time on potty chair should be increased. A treat should be given if the child sits as long or longer than he (she) sat the last time during the four regularly scheduled trips to the bathroom. (If the child fusses about being kept in the chair, allow him or her to get up.) The minimum time on potty applies during all six regularly scheduled trips to the bathroom (after getting up, before lunch, after nap, before dinner and two additional times).

Day 3:

Give treat for sitting on potty and increase daily minimum (equal or longer than time before) during the regularly scheduled trips to the bathroom. Give treats if minimum is achieved or elimination occurs.

Day 4:

Give treat for sitting on potty and increase daily minimum (equal or longer than time before) during the regularly scheduled trips to the bathroom. Give treats if minimum is achieved or elimination occurs.

Day 5:

Give treat for sitting on potty and increase daily minimum (equal or longer than time before) during the regularly scheduled trips to the bathroom. Give treats if minimum is achieved or elimination occurs.

Day 6:

Give treat for sitting on potty and increase daily minimum (equal or longer than time before) during the regularly scheduled trips to the bathroom. Give treats if minimum is achieved or elimination occurs.

Day 7:

Give treat for sitting on potty and increase daily minimum (equal or longer than time before) during the regularly scheduled trips to the bathroom. Give treats if minimum is achieved or elimination occurs.

Note: Days 1 through 7 of this first training week differ only in the minimum time requirements on the potty chair during the regularly scheduled trips. Do not keep your child on the potty over twelve minutes. During the first week give the reward when the child sits down as well as when he (she) passes the amount of time he (she) was on the potty the time before.

Second training week:

Whenever the child receives treats and praise for eliminating in the potty chair, continue saying the phrase "Come and tell Mommy when you have to _____." Even if the child is telling you when he (she) has to eliminate most of the time and is having very few accidents, continue to take him (her) to the bathroom the same number of times a day as before.

Days 8 through 14:

Continue procedure as for days 1 through 7 except increase the minimum time (as long or longer than time before—not to exceed twelve minutes—or until elimination occurs) during the regularly scheduled trips to the bathroom this week. Do *not* give treats for sitting down only for achieving time or elimination. Treat when the child wants to go to the bathroom or for letting you know before elimination occurs. Each time you reward the child say: "Call Mommy when you have to _____ in the potty." (When the child calls you, move quickly, especially during this week when control is being built.) Remember that approval should be delivered immediately.

It is advisable during the regularly scheduled trips to the bathroom to set a metal pan with small floating toys right on your son's (daughter's) lap and slowly fill it up with lukewarm water while encouraging him (her) to eliminate in the potty. (You can do this when the time on potty is at least four minutes.) The next trip to the bathroom after your child has achieved four minutes show him (her) the new game (do not wait this time until four minutes have elapsed but begin immediately after your child sits down). It is a good idea to have the pan and toys in the bathroom before achieving four minutes so that the child can play with them.

Third training week:

It is not necessary to ask the child if he (she) wants to go to the bathroom; in fact, this may slow down the training. Whenever you take the child to the bathroom for the regularly scheduled trips, continue to repeat the phrase, "When you _____ in the potty, it makes Mommy happy and you get _____ (name of treat)."

Increase liquid intake by giving an extra glass of juice, water, etc., between the trips to the bathroom. For the regularly scheduled trips to the bathroom stay with him (her) until elimination occurs or until twelve minutes has elapsed. Continue to reward longer times on the potty and when elimination occurs. If the child is coming to you and forewarning you that he (she) has to eliminate (at least occasionally), you can eliminate scheduled trips as the forewarnings become more frequent. Otherwise the procedure to follow remains the same as before. Continue to reward attempts to eliminate in the potty or coming to you and indicating in some way that elimination is about to occur.

Fourth training week:

Continue with the procedure as you have done during the preceding weeks. Reward an increase in amount of time on toilet during this week only if the child is not forewarning you over half the time. Continue to give the treat when elimination occurs in the proper place. Tell the child during this week that, "When you _____ in the potty it makes Mommy happy. You are a big boy (girl), etc."

Future training:

When the child is telling you he has to go to the toilet most of the time and is having fewer than two accidents per day, you may stop giving treats for successful performance unless he (she) asks for it, but continue to give praise. To evaluate check the child once per hour and record successes and accidents.

Scientific Application

Example 78

Pinpoint: *Aggressive hitting.*
                 (preschool boys, private kindergarten)

Record: Teacher complained boys went "out of control" during outside play periods (five children hurt in one week).

Consequate: Large punching bag dummy with red nose installed on play-ground.

Evaluate: No noticeable decrease in human hitting, six children hurt during week. Dummy punched frequently, especially in nose. (Actually, boys fought each other to take turns at dummy.)

Consequate II: Punching dummy removed. Individual boys isolated for duration of play period when observed hitting another child.

Evaluate II: After five days (seventeen isolations), hitting completely eliminated.

Note: Hitting, like other behavior, is *learned*. It is not a mystical entity deep inside everyone's system waiting to be released. The more children are reinforced for hitting, the more they will hit. Some people even develop a curious "self-fulfilling prophecy" in this regard. They sincerely believe that if they could just hit something they would feel much better. Thus, when frustrated, they hit something and, sure enough, they feel better. Parents may choose to reinforce behaviors such as "quiet play" following anger which are incompatible with hitting.

Professional Application

Example 79

Pinpoint:	*Arithmetic work in school.* (thirteen 6th grade boys, 12 and 13 years old)
Record:	Assignments completed during arithmetic period preceding recess averaged 4.2 (approximately nine incomplete assignments). Recess activity closely observed. All boys played 100% of the time during two-week period.
Consequate:	Boys told if assignments not completed, they could not go out to recess.
Evaluate:	Only four incidents of recess participation earned during the next week (three for one child). Arithmetic assignment completion did *not* increase following application of contingency.
Consequate II:	All boys instructed to work through recess and *denied* recess privilege; however, each boy allowed five minutes play in gym after finishing two arithmetic problems correctly.
Evaluate II:	Completed arithmetic assignments increased to nine by end of first week. By Tuesday of second week, all thirteen boys turned in assignments every day. After three weeks, accuracy reached an average of 80%.
Note:	This application represents a discrimination many adults fail to make. If the period of work is too long, the child cannot see the immediate rewards for his work; thus, behavior does not improve. It was apparent to the teacher that these thirteen boys (all slow in arithmetic) really enjoyed recess. The teacher used recess contingently, but it did not work. The time span of work without reward for these particular boys was too long. When the rewarding activity was given following a short period of work, they all produced—even though regular recess was denied. To keep the boys coming back from the gym rapidly, the teacher occasionally rewarded them immediately with another period in the gym for prompt return. By the end of the second week, all boys were running back from the gym to work again. When using activities as rewards, it is important to pay very close attention to "structuring activities in time." Many parents promise rewards which are desirable to the children but the work load is too long for the incentive to maintain the working behavior. The work at first may be reinforced after a small time and/or performance gains and the time span stretched after initial successful experiences.

Professional Application

Example 80

Pinpoint:	*Teaching lying behavior.* (11-year-old boy)
Record:	Known misconduct; boy observed stealing $1.00 from sister's bedroom.
Consequate:	Father took boy aside and with displeasure said, "Now, I want you to be honest with me, did you do it?"

Evaluate:

Lie 1   Child, "No."
         "Now, be honest!"
Lie 2   "No, I didn't do it."
         "Don't lie to me."
Lie 3   "I'm not, really I didn't do it."
         "I'm not going to tolerate any lying now."
Lie 4   "I'm not lying."
         "Why were you in there?"
Lie 5   "Where?"
         "The bedroom."
Lie 6   "Which bedroom?"
         "You know which bedroom."
Lie 7   "No, I don't."
         "Of course, you do."
Lie 8   "Dad, I really don't; I didn't do anything."
         "You took it."
Lie 9   "What?"
         "You know."
Lie 10   "I don't even have any money."
         "Ah! Who said anything about money?"
Lie 11   "You did."
         "No, I didn't."
Lie 12   "You said that I took Clara's money from her bedroom."
         "No, I didn't."
Lie 13   "Dad, I didn't take it."
         "How did you know it was money I was talking about?"
Lie 14   "I didn't."
         "You said, 'I didn't take Clara's money.' "
Lie 15   "No, I didn't say that."
         "What did you say?"
Lie 16   "I said, I didn't even know about Clara's money.' "
         "I'm not going to have you lie to me."
Lie 17   "I'm not lying, honest."
         "Now, once and for all, did you take it?"
Lie 18   "What?"
         "Clara's money."

Lie 19 "What money?"
       "I said I was not going to have any more lying."
Lie 20 "I'm not lying."
       etc., etc., etc., until

Truth 1 "Okay, okay, I did it."

Consequate II: Next morning. "Son, your behavior makes me very ashamed of you. You took your sister's money without her permission. Very few things are as serious as stealing, especially from a loved one. I choose not to give you the privilege of interacting with me or the family until you make retribution to Clara and this family. I know that you will think about this for a long, long time; I also know that you will pay back Clara and apologize to her and to the rest of us. I hope you can also think of a positive project that will demonstrate to us all the kind of person I know you are; right now you make us very, very sad."

Evaluate II: Boy exhibited "guilt" and engaged in project to earn back respect, i.e., positive familial interaction.

Note: Obviously consequate II should have been consequate I. Nothing is generally gained by playing detective or cross-examiner, except to increase lying. While most people can be caught in lies because they do not have good memories and/or are afraid and/or are young, this questioning process does not usually represent a very worthwhile pursuit. If the parent knows for certain that a child has committed an inappropriate act the parent should act on that basis. It does little good to get the child to admit it. If the parent is not sure, the parent should think through the possible consequences of the questioning process, i.e., to unwittingly teach lying.

Professional Application

Example 81

Pinpoint: *Positive piano practice.*
           (9-year-old girl)

Record: New behavior.

Consequate: Piano purchased with contingency child would (1) instruct self through two beginner books to earn privilege of taking lessons

Evaluate: and (2) pay part of earned allowance to piano teacher every lesson ($.25) for privilege of studying.

Evaluate: "Self-motivation" regarding practice—child practiced daily without admonition—three years.

Note: It was also decided in the above case to contract lessons through six-month periods with some weeks for rests, rather than just begin and act as though lessons might never stop. This obviates the need for children to view themselves as failures when they stop taking lessons. In music study it is curious that children must interpret their learning behavior as "defeat" when they have studied music successfully for from six months up to ten years. It should also be mentioned that six piano teachers were contacted before one was found who immediately realized the importance of accepting the quarter every lesson from the child. Another interesting note concerns the day this child came home and reported to her parents in stark disbelief that "Julie wants to stop taking lessons. And gosh! she doesn't even have to help pay for hers."

Professional Application

Example 82

Pinpoint: *Positive verbalizations about oneself and positive interaction with peers and parents.*
(16-year-old boy)

Record: Boy avoided peer interaction; stated he did not like himself because his parents couldn't stand him; stated he was not good and no one could possibly like him (self-records indicated over twenty times per day debased self and no positive peer or adult contact—two weeks' records).

Consequate: To teach good "self-concept" (appropriate self-labeling) boy instructed to (1) record positive verbalizations, (2) list hierarchy of interests and good points (himself and parents), (3) carry list in pocket and read list whenever he caught himself in self-abasement (incompatible response), (4) initiate peer

General Observation Form

PINPOINT *Talk negative about myself* Person(s) observed *Ben*

Observer(s) *Ben* Location *Any where at school*

Time of obs. *At school* Desire that behavior increase (decrease)

I (we) will conduct __*1*__ observations per *school day* every *day* for *2 wks.*
(number) (min-hr-day) (day-wk) (day-wk)

before consequating takes place.

Observation interval _____ Time between obs. _____
(sec-min-hr-day) (sec-min-hr-day)

RECORD Each occurrence of Pinpoint			CONSEQUATE Consequences following occurrence of behavior					EVALUATE Each occurrence of Pinpoint		
Date	Obs #	1 = neg. x = contacts	Date	Obs #	Approval *List read*	Dis-approval	Other *contact*	Date	Obs #	1 = neg. x = contacts
Mon.	1	𝍱𝍱𝍱𝍱	Mon.	1	𝍱𝍱𝍱		X	Mon.	1	11 XXXX
Tues.	2	𝍱𝍱𝍱 𝍱////	Tues.	2	𝍱𝍱𝍱 𝍱𝍱		—	Tues.	2	111 XXX
								Wed.	3	11 X
Wed.	3	𝍱𝍱𝍱 𝍱/	Wed.	3	𝍱𝍱𝍱////		X	Thurs.	4	— XXXXX
			Thurs.	4	𝍱𝍱𝍱𝍱		—	Fri.	5	11 —
Thurs.	4	𝍱𝍱𝍱 𝍱𝍱𝍱//	Fri.	5	𝍱𝍱𝍱/		X	Mon.	6	1 XXX
			Mon.	6	𝍱𝍱𝍱/		XX	Tues.	7	— XXXXX
Fri.	5	𝍱𝍱𝍱 𝍱///	Tues.	7	𝍱𝍱𝍱		XXX	Wed.	8	— XXXX
			Wed.	8	𝍱///		XXXXX	Thurs.	9	1 XXX
Mon.	6	𝍱𝍱𝍱	Thurs.	9	𝍱/		XXXX	Fri.	10	— XXXX
Tues.	7	𝍱𝍱𝍱 𝍱///	Fri.	10	//		XXXX			
Wed	8	𝍱𝍱𝍱 𝍱𝍱								
Thurs.	9	𝍱𝍱𝍱 𝍱𝍱𝍱								
Fri.	10	𝍱𝍱𝍱 𝍱///								

Total = *231* Totals = *124* *21* Total = *11* X = *32*
# Obs. = *10* # Obs. = *10*
Average = *23.1* When *I say good things* When *I say bad things* Average = *1.1*
(appropriate) (inappropriate)

Comments *Carried notebook at school. I also rate positive & negative reactions on 5-point scale and list what happened just before.*

for _____
(time-times)
Then these approvals will follow:
a. *feel good*
b. *think well*
c. *of self*

Then this disapproval will follow:
a. *Read list*

Summary:
Record total _____*231*
Evaluate total _____*11*
Record average _____*23.1*
Evaluate avg. _____*1.1*
Increase _____
Decrease _____*22.0*

contact (one per day) based on similar peer interests, (5) interact verbally with parents ten minutes per day in positive way.

Evaluate: One close friendship within six weeks (average three to four positive contacts daily); joined boy's science club. After three weeks he talked positively regarding parents.

Note: "Self-concept" usually relates to cognitive behavior and to a phenomenon called *labeling,* i.e., "I am a good person" as opposed to "I am no good" or "My child is a good person" versus "He is just a bad boy." Research regarding "labeling" seems quite conclusive in its implications regarding cause-and-effect relationships between labels and behavior. If a child gets the idea that he (she) is a "bad person," this will very probably influence his (her) behavior. That is, the child will behave in accordance with this "self-concept." One of the major theses of this book concerns the effect of positive as opposed to negative verbal expectations. For example, "I know you will do a good job" versus "Don't you dare try to cheat on your work." This is precisely what is meant by "catch the child being good and reward the child immediately." *Behavior that is reinforced increases.* If we catch children being good and reward them, we will probably have good children. If we only interact negatively with children, we create a negative cycle that is not only difficult to break but which probably actually produces more bad behavior.

Professional Application

Example 83

Pinpoint: *Fear of failure, worrying.*
(17-year-old girl)

Record: Girl reported, "worrying constantly." Mother recorded average of twelve times per day daughter talked about upcoming "problems."

Consequate: (1) Time set for fifteen minutes of daily worry. Must worry "hard" during this time, imagining all the bad things that might happen. (2) Rank ordered all possible outcomes of failure in upcoming events. (3) Instructed to say "stop," subvocally, every time worrying started during other times of day and change to organized study routine immediately after recording one instance of worrying on worry card carried by girl.

Evaluate: Worrying increased to "constantly" (daughter's own statement, no actual record). Worrying during prescribed time seemed "silly."

Consequate II: Girl told worrying had probably actually decreased from "constantly," had actual record been made, to point that she could discriminate between when she was or was not worrying; therefore, worry could be counted.

Evaluate II: Worrying decreased to twice daily; fifteen-minute worrying period decreased to five minutes (worry time became negative).

Note: Eventually the worrying time became extremely silly as girl leaned to plan constructive activities and worry time was discontinued.

Professional Application

Example 84

Pinpoint: *Striking children with objects.*
                  (9-year-old boy)

Record: Boy hit other children five times during four play periods.

Consequate: Adult assigned in vicinity. Boy praised and given doughnut after playing properly, although when boy hit someone, supervisor instructed to hit him back with same object. During second supervised play period, boy hit another child on the head with a plastic baseball bat. Immediately, the supervisor picked up the bat and hit the boy. Explanation to child: "When people are hit, it hurts."

Evaluate: Boy never observed hitting another child.

Note: This boy had been characterized by his parents as "having no conscience." Perhaps it would be more accurate to say that he did not realize the consequences of his own actions regarding pain. Parents later related that this same boy stopped with his hand in mid-air as he was going to strike his small brother and said, "I don't want to hurt you that much, I'm going to tell Daddy instead." We sometimes assume children have "learned" the consequences of their acts when, in fact, they merely know how to verbally relate (talk about) consequences of acts, which, of course, is not the same.

Professional Application

Example 85

Pinpoint:	*Excessive dawdling at school.* (5th grade class)
Record:	Three to five minutes to get "on-task" in individual study. (Average over eight days.)
Consequate:	Teacher instituted multiple divergent token systems. Some children received paper money which bought "surprise gifts" at end of day. Other children received candies on various time interval schedules. Some children accumulated points written in notebooks. Reinforcers changed constantly. Varying token reinforcers "stimulated interest and created mode of excitement in classroom."
Evaluate:	Individual dawdling decreased to approximately thirty seconds (average three days).
Note:	The children's expectation level increased general classroom excitement toward goal achievement (receiving tokens), which was later modified by stretching the time interval using only exchange tokens. If students have previously been on a single token system, sometimes it is wise to alter the routine. Changes in contingencies alone have been shown to increase "on-task" time and performance excellence. Parents may periodically desire to alter their system.

Professional Application

Example 86

Pinpoint: *Overweight child.*
                     (24-month-old child)

Record: Child 5 pounds heavy. Mother came upon child with food stolen
                     from refrigerator hidden under pile of newspapers with child
                     rapidly devouring food behind largest chair in corner of living
                     room.

Consequate: (1) Severe verbal disapproval for so much as touching re-
                     frigerator.
                     (2) Approval (very small candies) given for turning down food
                     between meals or second servings, e.g., "Oh, that's wonder-
                     ful, you don't want to be fat; here is a little bit."
                     (3) Instructed child in two classes of food: high calories—fat-
                     tening, low calories—not fattening. Child received lavish
                     verbal contact approval for correct discriminations when
                     asked by parents, family members, or relatives.
                     (4) Praised for leaving some food on plate.
                     (5) Child served one serving only (others in family with no
                     weight problems received many servings); child instructed
                     "to eat slowly so it will last."
                     (6) During each meal, some choices given to child, such as
                     between a little or a lot, high and low calorie foods: "I
                     know you want to eat some more of this, but will you?"
                     Correct choices reinforced with contact and praise.

Evaluate: Child's weight reduced in one year's time. No more food stolen.

Note: This child appeared to exhibit some self-control over eating be-
                     haviors previously though to be completely "out of hand." Many
                     times the child was present while family members ate. There-
                     fore, the father explained to the child the world isn't always
                     fair (teaching discriminations). Also this child received a great
                     deal of reinforcement at homes of friends and relatives for
                     knowledge about low and high calorie foods, as well as for turn-
                     ing down fattening foods. Parents often attempt to control
                     weight problems after many years of overeating (fat babies are
                     cute) rather than teaching discriminations early and reinforc-
                     ing correct choices which serve to control a potentially serious
                     problem.

Professional Application

Example 87

Pinpoint: *Physical abuse of mother.*
                 (15-year-old boy)

Record: Boy placed in country juvenile detention center for physical abuse of widowed mother, throwing her out of house, threatening others with a gun. Boy stated that he only wanted to play his guitar and be left entirely alone.

Consequate: (1) Guitar lessons contingent upon assigned work tasks. Guitar removed if tasks not completed. (2) Communication sessions developed between mother and son using boy's music as subject matter. Also, music paired with talk sessions to decrease high emotional responses. (3) Role playing sessions between counselor and mother to establish correct verbalizations.

Evaluate: Case terminated after four weeks (guitar was removed once); no beatings, arrests, or verbal abuses.

Note: The mother in this case was being unwittingly controlled by her son. In her words, "Everytime I try to talk with Fred and explain how I feel, he somehow turns my words against me and then goes into his room to listen to music; I am deeply concerned that he just doesn't understand me." Many parents, as the widow in this case, try to reason and explain their feelings, yet become "used" by their children. Reinforcing this insensitive child behavior is certainly unproductive for parents and does little but produce a kind of "sadism" in children. It seems extremely unproductive when parents allow children to use divorce, adoption, lack of love, sibling comparisons, etc., to get their way. In the above case the mother had fallen into the trap of "trying even harder to make her son understand her." It should be noted that after the boy's verbal and physical abuse stopped and he was rewarded for *appropriate* behavior (i.e., household duties, clearing the yard, not arguing, etc.), he did start to "understand" his mother.

Scientific Application

Example 88

Pinpoint: *Fighting during recess.*
                      (12-year-old boy)

Record: Teacher watched through window and recorded number of days
                      boy hit other children (four out of six days observed).

Consequate: Every time boy hit another child, he was taken into principal's
                      office and given one hard swat with paddle.

Evaluate: Playground fighting *increased* after consequences.

Consequate II: Procedures changed. Boy allowed talking privilege (five min-
                      utes) with principal every day he behaved well on playground.

Evaluate II: Fighting behavior decreased to zero over four weeks.

Note: Sometimes severe punishment can be actually rewarding to a
                      child. There are children who associate any attention given by
                      parents or authorities as indications of approval. (This is not as
                      absurd as it seems; remember, we discipline those we care
                      about.) Some children receive only negative attention. The ap-
                      plication of approval following *good* behavior changes this wrong
                      association.

Professional Application

Example 89

Pinpoint: *Non-caring (non-positive interaction with siblings).*
                      (9- and 6-year-old girls)

Record: Parents inadvertently overheard children's conversation. One
                      child wanted to be loving with sister, but problem child seemingly
                      without feeling (i.e., made completely insensitive negative state-
                      ments, such as "I don't care about you. I don't want to love you.
                      Leave me alone. I just want to play." When loving child dropped
                      her outstretched arms and started to cry the other said, "Cry
                      baby, cry baby, get away from me.")

Consequate: Parents set up verbal ostracism of "non-caring" child. No one
                      in family allowed to talk with child, touch, or "love her." Par-

ents did talk to each other in child's presence, "I wish Pam cared about other people and the rest of the family. I wish Pam wanted to be with the family and love us."

Evaluate: Child did not respond until third day; then asked to be talked to. Parents ignored, continued ostracizing until child's frequency for contact and verbal approval increased to "constantly." Parents continued to ignore but allowed sister to interact. After two days of intense approval interaction between sisters, parents began interacting again themselves.

Note: This case represents an *extreme* example of "withholding overt acts of love." The mother in this case was "terribly frightened because I thought we had a psychopath in the family. You just would not believe the cruelty of that conversation. It made me think I had some kind of monster." Perhaps some mothers overreact. It is assumed, however, that people do exist who "do not care." If caring and positive interaction is absent in a child, then it would seem wise for the child to learn it.

Professional Application

Example 90

Pinpoint: *Rebelliousness, disagreements, and refusal to talk to parents.* (11.5-year-old boy, large for age)

Record: Summer camp and school behavior in sharp contrast to misbehavior at home. (Young man reported camp and school misbehavior punished immediately; related interesting activities contingent on good behavior; therefore, no problem.) Boy indicated obedience only when father angry as father oblivious to misbehavior except when in a "sour mood."

Consequate: Counselor enlisted boy's aid in "experiments." Boy to be on lookout for situations when he could disagree or disobey, then to stop and imagine to himself that father was so angry he was ready to attack verbally and physically. It was explained that if he could control his behavior by imagining an angry father, probably he would not have to face an actual one. Role-playing practice in imagery produced reactions similar to when he actually faced an angry father. Further treatment focused on the boy accepting authority of his father, even when unreasonable.

Evaluate:

Home situation improved. First nine days boy reported using the "little trick" anywhere from ten to twenty-five times. The first week father had even taken him to an auto show and spent an enjoyable day. (It was pointed out that present obedience and restriction in freedom would result in more freedom later—delay of gratification.) Following some weeks boy took father more into account (turned down volume on record player so it wouldn't disturb father, etc.). During the fourth week an argument developed which was so violent the boy didn't want to return home. Father stayed away from boy for awhile with improvement in relations continuing. Boy received more freedom; it became unnecessary to use "imagining father angry" technique as father became more reasonable and son less inclined to disagree on every little thing.

Note:

A professional behavioral therapist helped this boy over a five-month period. The most significant factor appears to be that the boy, by pretending the father was angry, was able to tell himself that disobedience would lead to disapproval. This method of having children "talk to themselves and imagine potentially good or bad results" is a method of assisting in the development of self-control especially if the thoughts are immediately followed by approval. This technique can be enhanced as parents teach children to "label" many aspects of their behavior and follow the reproduction with approval. The results may not be as dramatic as the present case where the use of a thought "trick" improved a terrible home situation, but with continued communication parents are able to assist children in self-control procedures.

Scientific Application

Example 91

Pinpoint:

Use of illegal drugs.
(19-year-old boy)

Record:

"Pot," two to three times weekly; LSD, two occurrences.

Consequate:

Boy began research on effects of drugs and was paid $5.00 for each two-page paper written.

Evaluate: LSD discontinued.

Note: This boy stated he found what he considered good evidence for discontinuing LSD but found conflicting evidence on the dangers of marijuana, so he decided not to stop. Many other young people with same contingencies have decided to give up all drugs because of legal, occupational, and/or societal consequences. Many parents may desire to emphasize preventative measures stressing what they feel to be more important issues than the medical effects of drugs. In these preventative programs, rewards are given for research concerning laws, community employment, church, and legal views.

Professional Application

Example 92

Pinpoint: *Juvenile offender.*
                    (14-year-old boy)

Record: Many disruptions at home—came before court on two separate occasions: one theft, one ungovernable charge.

Consequate: Summer vacation: spending money contingent upon no more offenses and finishing summer school.

Evaluate: No arrests, although summer school not finished.

Consequate II: Boy placed in Detention Center during family's vacation.

Evaluate II: Boy left home, went to live with friend's parents.

Consequate III: Kicked out after four weeks—moved to another friend's parents.

Evaluate III: Kicked out after thirteen days—went traveling.

Consequate IV: Called father long distance (collect) for money to come home; received money but did not come home.

Evaluate IV: Unknown.

Note: In this case the juvenile was placed by his counselor in the County Detention Center during the family's two-week vacation. It was only then he began to believe that he could not get his own way and thus wanted to live elsewhere. It should be noted that although this boy had just failed all prescribed contingencies regarding summer school work, his parents still planned to take him on vacation in order to "develop a fresh rapport." The above juvenile court counselor reported many failures because of well-intended parents who allow children's friends to live with them after these children have run away or been purposely ostracized by their own parents. Usually such well-intended parents believe that they "understand" these children better. To allow youngsters to live with one without the express consent of their parents constitutes gross irresponsibility, not charity.

Professional Application

Example 93

Pinpoint:	*Excessive sleeping.* (college daughter)
Record:	Average time sleeping 9.5 hours per night; complaints to parents of "not enough study time."
Consequate:	Behaviors such as taking a shower, putting on lounging pajamas, putting up hair, etc., *eliminated* from early evening routine. Substituted study, activity time followed by thirty-minute pleasurable or relaxing time as reward just before bed.
Evaluate:	Sleep time reduced to seven hours (average over three weeks). Girl reported an increase in general well-being and also more studying.
Note:	This study is an example of self-control, i.e., controlling aspects of one's environment which in turn will tend to help control us. The elimination of behaviors normally associated with going to bed early in the evening as well as planning an activity which would both reinforce increased studying, as well as keep one awake to enjoy the activity just preceding bedtime, were arranged by the girl.

Professional Application

Example 94

Pinpoint: *Teaching contractual agreements.*
                  (9th grade civics class)

Record: Nothing.

Consequate: Beginning of term each student wrote a contract including
                  amount of work to be completed for special class project as
                  well as evaluation criteria for determining student's grade. In-
                  dividual contracts exchanged among students. Entire class then
                  chose a project and wrote one contractual agreement determin-
                  ing individual and collective responsibilities, including penalties
                  for "illegal" behaviors. Teacher assumed role of interested by-
                  stander as students pursued class project. Disputes during course
                  of project adjudicated in "class court" (some students did not
                  do their share of work).

Evaluate: Effective learning judged by teacher on basis of ex post facto
                  essays written by students.

Note: It is interesting that the predominant theme of most essays
                  concerned "fairness." Written contractual agreements are very
                  effective for this age group and may concern any cause-and-
                  effect relationship between the parties (teacher/student, parent/
                  student). Contracts specify contingenies ("If I do my work you
                  promise to pay me," etc.) and may be used for individual's
                  and/or groups. Exactly the same benefits accrue from such writ-
                  ten contracts as from similar, more sophisticated, adult agree-
                  ments. Many families have found teen-agers to be especially
                  responsive to this method of teaching cause-and-effect relation-
                  ships.

Professional Application

Example 95

Pinpoint: *Vomiting following dates.*
                  (18-year-old girl)

Record: Girl reported vomiting attacks every morning following either
                  a weekend date or weekday date (three months' duration).

Consequate: Series of dating behaviors planned starting with situations ex-
trememly divergent from normal dating conditions. Began with
short one-hour dates, then time and involvement steadily increased for two weeks until dating situations more closely ap-
proximated "normal" dates with involvement (private locale,
physical signs of affection, etc.). Girl kept a log of dating activities to discriminate dating sequence and provide discriminations
across time for future dating behaviors.

Evaluate: Vomiting attacks eliminated following five hours with counselor (two weeks of dating) and girl returned to normal dating
pattern.

Note: One-year follow-up indicated only one vomiting attack had
occurred which was attributed to the flu. The investigator in this
case speculated that a date-sleep-vomit association had inadvertently been reinforced. The learned association to dating was
changed by beginning with behaviors distant enough from regular dating to learn new date-not-sleep-not-vomit association
and then bringing dating behaviors closer and closer by successive approximations toward regular dating behaviors. This
same procedure may be used to change other negative associations. Start with behaviors similar but distant enough not to produce negative reaction. Gradually by successive approximations
get closer to the desired goal either spatially (getting closer and
closer across time) or topographically (closer and closer to
similar behaviors). When dealing with severe reactions, if the
undesired behavior doesn't change with two tries seek a professional behavioral therapist.

Scientific Application

Example 96

Pinpoint: *Negative verbalizations.*
(three girls—9, 12, and 14 years old)

Record: One hundred nineteen occurrences in one week counted during afternoons and evening by mother.

Consequate: (Negative modeling.) Bad examples illustrated using TV com-
mercials (e.g., "My wash is whiter than your wash." "Isn't

General Observation Form

PINPOINT *Using negative comments* Person(s) observed *Sitka, Cathrio,* *Machelle*

Observer(s) *Mother*   Location *around house*

Time of obs. *4:00 – 9:00 p.m.*   Desire that behavior increase (decrease)

I (we) will conduct ___*1*___ observations per *day* every *day* for *7 days*
  (number)   (min-hr-day)   (day-wk)   (day-wk)
before consequating takes place.

Observation interval ___*5 hours*___   Time between obs. *24 hours*
        (sec-min-hr-day)   (sec-min-hr-day)

RECORD — Each occurrence of Pinpoint			CONSEQUATE — Consequences following occurrence of behavior					EVALUATE — Each occurrence of Pinpoint		
Date	Obs #		Date	Obs #	Approval modeling sessions	Dis-approval	Other	Date	Obs #	
3/20	1	𝍸𝍸𝍸	3/27	1	𝍸𝍸𝍸			4/24	1	1
3/21	2	𝍸𝍸𝍸 𝍸𝍸	4/3	2	𝍸𝍸𝍸			4/25	2	11
3/22	3	𝍸𝍸𝍸 𝍸𝍸	4/10	3	𝍸𝍸𝍸 𝍸𝍸			4/26	3	—
3/23	4	𝍸𝍸𝍸 𝍸𝍸𝍸	4/17	4	𝍸𝍸𝍸 𝍸𝍸			4/27	4	—
3/24	5	𝍸𝍸𝍸 𝍸𝍸𝍸						4/28	5	1
3/25	6	𝍸𝍸𝍸 𝍸𝍸𝍸						4/29	6	1
3/26	7	𝍸𝍸𝍸 𝍸𝍸𝍸 𝍸𝍸						4/30	7	—

Total = *118*   Totals = *37*   Total = *5*
\# Obs. = *7*   \# Obs. = *7*
Average = *16.9*

When *girls say kind things* (appropriate)   When *girls say neg. things* (inappropriate)

Average = *16.9*

Comments *Girls now are praising each other and telling each how kind the others are.*

for *each time* (time-times)
Then these approvals will follow:
a. *words spoken*
b. *praise*
c. ___

Then this disapproval will follow:
a. *ignored by all*

Summary:
Record total ___*118*
Evaluate total ___*5*
Record average ___*16.9*
Evaluate avg. ___*0.7*
Increase ___
Decrease ___*113*
per week

Average = *0.7*

149

Gladys fat, oh! here she comes . . . Hi Gladys." "Honey, it just won't work—I've tried that old (product) time and time again. Okay, have it your way—you'll see." (later) "See I told you so, you never listen." "Husbands can't do anything—let me do it—*see,*" etc.

Evaluate: Girls began to become sensitized to their verbalizations and actually started keeping records to help each other decrease such "nasty" comments. Mother counted only five comments during the fifth week.

Note: Television provides an excellent source for both positive and negative behaviors. TV can be used to sensitize as well as shape both appropriate and inappropriate behaviors. Parents must be present, however, if they want to take part in the definition.

Professional Application

Example 97

Pinpoint: *Child uses adoption to control parents.*
                    (16-year-old girl)

Record: Girl used statements concerning her adoption to "get her way." Engaged parents in "proving their love" and providing "payoff" (seven instances in one month).

Consequate: Parents instructed to ignore all talk concerning adoption, to leave girl's presence when subject brought up unless girl verbalized approval statements, and to prepare for extreme test.

Evaluate: Girl ran away; she returned the following weekend.

Consequate II: Girl instructed by parents that parental approval would continue to be contingent upon good behavior not genetic involvement.

Evaluate II: The use of "adoption" to control parents ceased.

Note: Many children at all ages use parental concern, worry, or guilt to change parent's behavior. The child learns one of several perverted associations. "When I get punished and act hurt long enough someone will give in," i.e., good things happen after I suffer. "My parents love me so if I act nasty long enough they'll give up," i.e., to stop the negative behavior parents provide pay-off. This reinforces parents as obnoxious behavior stops, but children are reinforced for persisting in negative behavior for longer and longer periods. "When I get their goat anything is libel to happen," i.e., child's payoff *is* the anger of parents.

Professional Application

Example 98

Pinpoint: *Walking in street.*
                (1.5- to 4-year-old boys and girls)

Record: Various occurrences (parent's self-report).

Consequate: Children spanked, yelled at for going into street, given approval for verbalizing comments concerning "not going into street"; taken to edge of pavement and taught discrimination if pre-verbal, i.e., child put on grass, given approval taken barely onto pavement spanked, yelled at. Child taught that when they hold parents' hands then and only then may they walk in or across streets, parking lots, etc.

Evaluate: ?

Note: The strength of reinforcement required for teaching should be in direct proportion to the danger involved. (It seems unwise to put both dirty hands and potential death into the same "no-no" basket.) Sometimes complete supervision or instilling fear is the early alternative to potential danger; sometimes teaching for discrimination is advisable (i.e., concerning knives, hot stoves, scissors, electricity, poisons, water, etc.). *The parent must decide what is important.*

Professional Application

Example 99

Pinpoint:	*Noncooperation in school.* (11th grade, English, five boys ages 16–17)
Record:	No English assignments completed during two-week period. Students also refused to recite orally. Boys caught "shooting craps" in back of room.
Consequate:	All boys sent to principal's office and given a "good talking to" concerning classroom responsibilities and advantages of learning English.
Evaluate:	No change occurred in behavior. Boys became more noncooperative and began to mimic female teacher. Caught shooting craps twice during following week.
Consequate II:	Teacher began to praise every class member who cooperated in giving oral recitations from selected literature.
Evaluate II:	No change noted. Not one boy volunteered to participate in oral recitations. Teacher saw dice once but didn't catch boys in any games.
Consequate III:	Everyone who participated in oral recitations allowed to bring any book or magazine to class for thirty minutes of private reading.
Evaluate III:	One noncooperative boy brought a *Playboy* magazine to teacher after class and asked sarcastically: "If I read aloud from your book, can I read mine?" Teacher agreed. Next class session he did. Within four weeks all boys recited.
Note:	The teacher was also able to shift these boys' interest from *Playboy* to *Hot Rod,* and after four months to sophisticated sports magazines found in school library. This case demonstrates effective use of peer contingencies and approximations toward better literature through lack of censorship. Parents should be aware of school interactions and also not hide from their children's problems in this everchanging world. Parents who censor communication topics with older children insure that values and attitudes may be taught by others with no chance for input, correction, or feedback from the home environment.

Professional Application

Example 100

Pinpoint: *Bad attitude.*
                (6-year-old boy)

Record: Child continued maladaptive responses just a little past point of instruction. Thus, when adult (teacher) said, "Stop talking," he did, but continued *almost* to point of being disobedient. When adult said, "Do not pick the flowers," he picked leaves. When she said, "Come here," he walked very slowly. When she said, "Quiet down," he did—still slightly louder than the group but not so loud as to receive punishment. This child (like so many others) delicately balanced upon the "edge of propriety." Punishment seemed not quite warranted, and reward seemed ridiculous.

Consequate: Teacher set up short lesson using *vicarious modeling.* Three names not duplicated in close friendships were presented. Child was presented a new word, *attitude.* Teacher paired names with the new word: George has a *bad attitude,* Sam has an *all right attitude,* Tommy has a *good attitude.* When their mother tells these three boys, "Let's all pick up the mess," George tries to get out of work or hides his mess in the desk, Sam cleans up his own mess only, but Tommy cleans up his own mess and then helps the other children. The teacher talked through two such specific examples, then let the child say what he thought George, Sam, and Tommy would do. (Children are usually very correct in these assessments, especially as they describe their own problems.) Teacher made several praising comments, stating, "I like Tommy the very, very best." She then asked problem boy whom he would want for a friend. (The teacher now had a word, *attitude,* that she could use to describe this boy's behavior in specific and general contexts, "That's a good attitude, Cort.") She now began rewarding *good attitudes* instead of being frustrated at not being able to find responses to deal with this child.

Evaluate: Child in question changed "attitude" when rewarded for proper verbal and motoric behavior.

Professional Application

Example 101

Pinpoint: *Teaching beginning reading.*
                       (ten research studies employing 400 children: retarded, slow
                       readers, and unselected kindergarten and 1st graders)

Record: Reading scores assessed prior to reading instruction.

Consequate: Programmed reading for periods of up to one semester.

Evaluate: No tutored children failed to read with exception of one "nor-
                       mal" first grader and some (but not all) children with I.Q.s
                       below 50. One experiment showed relatively rapid acquisition
                       of reading vocabulary by simple pairing of words with pictures.
                       In another study, retarded children taught reading vocabulary
                       to other retarded children with simple tutoring program. In
                       other research, sight-reading vocabulary taught in sentence con-
                       texts to slow readers, retarded, and normal children. Two ex-
                       tension studies showed frequent alternation of programmed
                       tutoring and classroom teaching more effective than less frequent
                       alternation. One study indicated reinforcement proportion ap-
                       proximately 20% more effective than higher levels.

Note: It appears that after approval has been established as an incen-
                       tive, periodic withholding of approval develops a "hope" which
                       is more effective than when the adult reinforces all the time.
                       The interested parent can find literally hundreds of experiments
                       in scientific journals concerning the effects of various reinforce-
                       ment schedules. The central issues related to programmed in-
                       structions seem little different from any other learning sequence.
                       One should begin where the child is. Learning steps should be
                       small, and adequate reinforcement techniques (including feed-
                       back) should be employed. Every parent can individualize con-
                       tingencies and follow systematic procedures.

Scientific Application

Example 102

Pinpoint: *Soiling in pants (encopresis).*
(9-year-old boy)

Record: Mother reported soiling from one to four times daily for four years (same record for fourteen days of observation).

Consequate: Mother instructed to ignore soiling (formerly she washed, changed, and gave boy a great deal of attention). Boy had to change himself, wash himself, and also received *no* attention from mother.

Evaluate: Soiled once first day, once on twenty-fourth day, and not again during ninety days of observation.

Note: This lad had also complained a great deal of physical ailments. Mother had been instructed to ignore these complaints; however, this was unnecessary as they dropped out along with the soiling.

Scientific Application

Example 103

Pinpoint: *Temper outbursts.*
(4-year-old boy, recorded I.Q. 72 and 80, possible brain damage)

Record: Frequency of objectionable behaviors varied from 18 to 113 during sixteen one-hour periods (sticking out tongue, kicking, yelling, threatening to remove clothing, calling people names, throwing objects, biting, and hitting self).

Consequate: Consequences applied by mother in home two to three times per week for six one-hour sessions. Researchers helped mother by giving signals indicating: (1) she should tell her son to stop doing what he was doing, or (2) place him in isolation for five minutes, or (3) give approval (attention, praise, and affection).

Evaluate: Rate of objectionable behavior decreased (range one to eight per session). Isolation used four times; special attention given ten times.

Consequate II: No signals given; mother told to "act as before."

Evaluate II: Objectionable behaviors increased, but ranged well below orig-
                    inal recordings (two to twenty-four per session). It appeared
                    mother "learned." She reported more self-assurance, increased
                    attention, delivered firm commands, and did not give in after
                    denying a request.

Consequate III: Consequate I reinstated, except special attention for desirable
                    play excluded.

Evaluate III: Objectionable behavior again *decreased* (almost identical to
                    consequate I, ranging two to eight per session).

Note: No contact was maintained with the mother for twenty-four
                    days after completion of project. She was given no instructions
                    as to how to act and was given complete freedom to use any
                    technique she desired. Later, a three-session post contact check
                    was made. Even after this long interval, the behaviors considered
                    objectionable were still very low. The mother reported her
                    child was well-behaved and less demanding. Isolation was used
                    on the average of once per week. The mother's attitude toward
                    her son was also considered to be more approving. This excel-
                    lent well-controlled scientific study was conducted in the home
                    by the mother. Many mothers feel "guilty" about parent/child
                    interaction and try many solutions but do not have accurate
                    records as to results of the "new" procedures. This study indi-
                    cates the confidence of the mother increased when she found,
                    from records, the results of her behavior. Any parents may
                    achieve similar results. Changes in behavior may not always
                    coincide with expectations, but the parent who keeps records
                    will have the courage to try again without "guilt."

Scientific Application

Example 104

Pinpoint: *School failure.*
                    (twelve 11- to 14-year-old students)

Record: Each student failed at least two academic subjects.

Consequate: Individual work-play routines developed by teachers and par-
                    ents. Students given special after-school assignments (approxi-

mately thirty minutes). Work immediately checked by parents and points assigned. Points totaled each day to "buy" privileges and things (TV watching, outside peer playtime, two children received money, one child—supper, one student—Saturday hiking plus one TV program nightly, one student—time using "ham radio"). Time ratio for work-play approximately four to one in most cases. Thus, thirty minutes "on-task" work carried points worth two hours of activity or other reward.

Evaluate:

Eleven of twelve students improved (average increase 1.5 letter grades in four months). One fourteen year old ran away from home; this student entirely on money contingency; later parents admitted they began to pay him before, rather than after, study sessions, i.e., he was manipulating them, rather than doing his work.

Note:

This program is effective, but demands parental consistency. Many students will respond to such a program when parents: (1) admit their child has a problem, (2) have some confidence in the school (teacher/counselor), and (3) will be honest in dispensing rewards. Parents have often initiated such programs in cooperation with school personnel.

Professional Application

Example 105

Pinpoint:

Assessing truth.
(twelve children, all under 6 years old)

Record:

Children suspected of wrong-doing, i.e., in this particular case parent entered room of two children after younger brother started to cry (parent's self-report).

Consequate:

"Annabelle story" (or masculine counterpart name) instituted. Child given story paradigm which initially described a little boy or girl with all aspects of child's own physical features, home environment, etc. After this initial programming, the suspected wrong is then recounted vicariously. For example, "Cherrie, you have such nice blue eyes, and you are such a big four year old with nice toys and a little brother. I am going to tell you a story. There once was a girl named Annabelle. She had pretty blue eyes and she was a big four year old. Annabelle also had a little brother. One day Annabelle was playing with her little brother, and Annabelle's mother heard the little brother crying. Why do you think Annabelle's brother was crying?"

Evaluate: Cherrie, "Because he took Annabelle's toy, and Annabelle hit him."

Note: This procedure works almost always with young children because children of this age do not have the power to think abstractly. It is often extremely difficult for parents to believe that children do not realize they are describing themselves.

Professional Application

Example 106

Pinpoint: *Constant talking out and disturbing others during study time.* (15-year-old boy, math class)

Record: On-task study behavior ranged from 3 to 45% with an average of approximately 25%.

Consequate: Boy took daily report card for teacher to check. Teacher marked yes or no to such items as acceptable use of class time; assignments completed on time; homework assignments; overall behavior good. When student earned all yesses, he received snacks, TV, and permission to go outdoors. Even one "no" resulted in loss of privileges. (Child lived in a foster home for predelinquent boys.)

Evaluate: Study behavior rose to 95%; it remained high for six days of observation.

Consequate II: Student no longer received teacher's checks; he was told he would be granted privileges anyway.

Evaluate II: Study time dropped to 25% the first day, 10% the second day, and boy also got into one fight.

Consequate III: Privileges again made contingent on card signatures.

Evaluate III: Study time increased to 80% first day, dropped for three days until teacher assigned one "no" whereupon on-task study time increased to 100% and remained high for remainder of term.

Note: This well-controlled scientific study (one of three within the same article using trained observers) indicates that home-based rewards can maintain on-task school behavior. Rewards were on a daily basis as it was necessary for the teacher as well as foster-parents to "prove" that they would, or could, be consistent. When no card was required behavior was disruptive; however, the teacher also had to assign a "no" before the lesson had been learned.

                  A subsequent experiment indicated that when cards were given only two days per week (reducing daily rewards) this also maintained a high level of appropriate behavior in class.

Scientific Application

Example 107

Pinpoint: *Embarrassment.*
                  (three 15-year-old girls, high school music class)

Record: Self-evaluation indicated students possessed "no musical talent." Students refrained from individual singing, stating "My voice sounds funny" or "I cannot carry a tune."

Consequate: Two-fold program to: (1) teach all students discrimination between possessing ability and performing before class, and (2) teach entire class role-playing to deliver approval feedback to "insecure students."

Evaluate: Students learned to participate in activities, even though they did not possess even moderate "talent." Class also taught to smile, nod heads, keep eye contact, and approvingly reinforce a terrible performance. Teacher played role of extremely poor singer while class learned to "put a performer at ease" by *not* responding to performer's fear and avoidance with fear and avoidance, but with approving reinforcement. Shy performers began participating regularly. One girl stated: "I have always known I've a lousy voice, but now I love to sing."

Note: Students in upper grades who have a problem with embarrass-
                    ment in relation to any activity have *learned* this embarrassment
                    from someone. It is usually learned traumatically. For ex-
                    ample, the young child sings and enjoys himself until one day
                    he shockingly learns his voice sounds terrible, whereupon he
                    stops singing. Unfortunately, many adults do not understand the
                    importance of teaching discriminations, and therefore continu-
                    ously prepare many youngsters for disillusionment, some for
                    catastrophe. Dedicated to well-intended censorship, many par-
                    ents pretend that no one is different from anyone. "Celia has
                    only one arm, but in my eyes she has two just like everyone
                    else." "Fred has a lisp, but I ignore his impediment." "Spencer
                    is a Negro, but among good people everyone's skin is the same."
                    It is unfortunate that these children must get out in the world
                    where other children do not censor: "Hey Celia, what happened
                    to your arm?" "Gosh, Fred, you talk funny." "Why are your
                    hands white, Spencer?" Some children even make fun of these
                    differences. Yet where can children learn to accept differences
                    proudly and not make fun? Certainly not in a school or home
                    where differences *do not exist*. Children can easily be taught dis-
                    crimination of differences. Much more important, they can be
                    taught *acceptance* and *respect* for differences. This learning,
                    however, will not come from censorship.

Professional Application

Example 108

Pinpoint: *Obesity*.
                    (ages 10 through 52, sixty-four individuals, 5 to 57 pounds
                    overweight where medical examination revealed no medical
                    problem and physician supervised medical aspects of diets)

Record: Many environment stimuli, as well as some bodily responses
                    (emotions), generally become connected with eating in previous
                    history of overweight person. (Many of us eat when we get
                    angry or perhaps when we are sad or just plain tired, "I always
                    feel better if I have something to eat.") In addition certain activi-
                    ties are generally associated with eating or drinking—television

viewing, fixing meals, "I have to see what it tastes like," in coffee breaks, hard work, "A cold beer sure tastes good after working," cocktail parties, "I really shouldn't but just to be sociable," card parties, and so on. Generally many normal everyday activities are habitually associated with food or liquid intake.

Consequate: Instructions given to obese:

1. *Eating place*

The first step is to designate a place (specific chair at specific table) where eating will occur. This place should be maintained with rare exceptions until your weight is down. Engage only in eating at that particular place (i.e., no reading, studying, working, playing). Henceforth, this is your *eating place*. All meals, snacks, and drinks (other than water or low-calorie liquids) should be consumed in that location.

2. *Eat on purpose*

Most of us have become used to engaging in many other behaviors other than eating during meal or snack time. People talk, work, play, watch, listen, and exercise at the very same time they eat. Weight control under these conditions is very difficult. Therefore, discriminations need to be made. To build discriminations one must *eat on purpose*. Do not be distracted from eating in the "eating place." You should contemplate every spoonful, forked morsel, or swallow. The easiest way is to talk to yourself about eating as it occurs. This is behavior incompatible with many other behaviors during mealtime. As you look at a morsel of food you say, "Now I'm going to cut my meat. I must pick up my knife and fork and cut my meat so I can eat it. Now I'm picking up my knife and fork, and now I am cutting my meat so it can be eaten. I lay down my knife, pick up my meat, and take it to my mouth." Stop just before the food gets to the mouth and say, "This meat is now going to be chewed and swallowed." Place the food in the mouth and think about chewing the food and say, "Now I am chewing my food" (chew twenty times saying how good the food is), next as you swallow say, "Now I have swallowed the food, and I am going to get the benefit from that bit of food." This procedure should be followed every meal for a period of two weeks before any diet is started. This procedure ensures that food taken into the mouth will get into the mouth *on purpose*. This also serves to bring eating behavior under control of your intentions and to break learned connections between eating and other behaviors. It also slows the rate of eating.

3. *Obesity chart*

During the two weeks that you eat on purpose in your designated place take your morning nude weight every day at the same time (preferably just after getting up in the morning). Construct a large chart which in large letters at the top reads: OBESITY CHART. Record your weight every day. The best procedure is to have someone watch you weigh who should check the scales and make a comment about how fat you look ("Look at those rolls around your stomach; your hips are not very nice looking when you are so fat," etc.). The two-week chart will give you a baseline from which to measure progress and the person (mother, spouse, sister, etc.) will give added incentive to reduce. Make certain the chart is attached to the wall in a prominent place where you can see it as you get ready for the day's activities. Some people also find it helpful to include a measurement chart (waist, etc.).

4. *Breakfast*

Breakfast should be considered a reward for looking neat and clean. A sloppy appearance is conducive to gaining weight (even though you stay at home). Wear clean clothes and engage in appropriate sprucing. Men should shave and be neat even on days off, and women should put on makeup every morning before breakfast.

5. *Diet sarcasm card*

A small card with sarcastic comments relating to eating should be typed, carried with you and read before, during, and after every meal; also, whenever you feel hungry during the day. Such a card might contain the following statements:

  a. I enjoy eating more than feeling good.
  b. It is fun to be overweight; everyone enjoys looking at me.
  c. Fat persons are so likeable they receive many invitations for dates from neat people.
  d. High blood pressure doesn't bother me because it is better than losing weight.
  e. I could never have a heart attack. It only happens to those other fat people.
  f. It is so pleasant to wear my dresses that are as large as tents. In fact, I may develop until I can get work in a circus.

6. *Eating cue*

Use something at the table that is always present when you eat. For example, use a small hourglass or brightly colored napkin or conspicuous charm (any brightly colored object will do). When you sit down to eat take the object, place it in view, and say, "This gives me permission to eat," then read the card, look at the object, and go through the *eating on purpose* routine. This object with the card gives a carryover to other situations, and you may come to feel guilty if it is not being used.

7. *Eat off schedule*

Schedule meals at variable times during the day and stick to your *variable schedule*. If other members of the family are unable to meet your schedule, then it is better to eat by yourself. *This does not mean to snack between your variable schedule.*

8. *Calorie chart*

Every morsel of food should be logged with number of calories as it is eaten on an intake chart which shows your quota for each day.

9. *Additional helps*

    a. If you shop, shop by list only, and never allow yourself to buy anything which is not on your list.
    b. Prepare the shopping list immediately after dinner.
    c. Food should be out of sight when beginning the program except when actually eating or preparing meals.
    d. One-half hour before each mealtime take a small 6 oz. glass of juice or appropriate liquid. Thus, you will probably not be as hungry when mealtime arrives.
    e. Remember to get your diet from a doctor and stay under his supervision during your program.

Evaluate: All individuals lost weight (average 15 lbs.) from following the above procedures. In combination these procedures are extremely effective; some people report weight loss by using just one of the above. Proper body weight is much like most other aspects of life, it usually takes discipline.

Scientific Application

Example 109

Pinpoint: *Children manipulating parents.*
(three children, 6-year-old boy attempted to force parents to comply with his wishes, 4-year-old boy considered excessively dependent at home and aggressive in nursery school, 4-year-old boy extremely stubborn in presence of mother but not with other adults)

Record: Each mother observed while interacting with son.

Consequate: Mothers instructed: (1) in delivery of approval techniques,
                   (2) to ignore inappropriate behavior, and (3) to respond with
                   praise and affection for appropriate behavior. Mother *A* re-
                   sponded positively to child *only* when he did not attempt to force
                   compliance. Mother *B* ignored child's dependency and re-
                   sponded approvingly to independent behavior. Mother *C* ig-
                   nored oppositional behavior and responded to cooperating
                   behavior. Later, Mother *C* instructed to isolate son in empty
                   room for at least five minutes immediately following opposi-
                   tional responses.

Evaluate: First two boys' behavior improved markedly through the moth-
                   ers' attention to appropriate behavior and ignoring inappropri-
                   ate responses. The third boy improved only after isolation.

Note: This is a good example of differential treatment. The parents
                   should always remember that it is necessary to structure for
                   each child. It should be noted that the use of disapproval (iso-
                   lation) was necessary for one child before improvement took
                   place.

Scientific Application

Example 110

Pinpoint: *Developing a study routine.*
                   (thirty-six teen-age students, girls and boys)

Record: Average grade level considered by both teachers and parents to
                   be at least one letter grade below potential (average grades =
                   C−).

Consequate: Students asked to indicate amount of time each felt appropriate
                   to achieve goal (raising grades). Total time indicated cut by
                   40%, after which contract signed by pupil, teacher, and parent.
                   Specific routines developed to aid in concentration:

                   1. *Underlining*
                   First it was explained that learning to underline or to outline
                   were *not* the same as learning assigned material (many students
                   have developed negative reactions particularly to these two ac-

tivities). If students want to learn to draw lines it should be done with many colored pencils, a ruler, and blank paper. If students want to outline, the daily paper will do just as well as school material.

2. *Concentration*

The important aspects of study are *on-task* concentration and repetition of materials not fully learned (asking oneself questions and answering as the material is studied—talking to oneself). On-task study time determined by each student before beginning to study material. Students also noted number of their distracting thoughts (no student able to complete *six* minutes of study time with fewer than eight distraction marks). On-task study time increased in following manner: Each student purchased a timer (kitchen timer, $4.00 to $7.00) with his own money and set aside only weekday study times which fit individual schedule (weekends free from nagging parents appealed to all students).

3. *Study place*

Students chose a "study-place" where only study would take place. If necessary, other members of family used the same spot, but the student with the problem could study only there and nowhere else in the house. A straight-backed chair was chosen with attempts made to place chair facing a corner or blank wall. Prominent signs were constructed warning family members (including parents) to stay away during study time. Distractions such as music (radios, "hi fi") eliminated (these do *not* increase studying effectiveness). Only one book or one set of materials taken to study place for each study session.

4. *Distraction cards*

Students used 5 x 8 inch cards labeled as to date, time started, time finished, session number as well as open space for distractions (distracting thoughts or interruptions). Students chose a pleasant activity to engage in during break times (reading, eating, listening to radio, talking with friends, telephone calls, etc.), got materials ready, removed watches and other indicators of time, filled in above card, set kitchen timer for six minutes, and began to study. Whenever the student was distracted in any way (defined by student to help teach discrimination between on-task and off-task behavior), the student marked in space provided for distractions and also wrote in longhand at the bottom of card, "Get back to work." After having first noticed a distraction (competing sound, daydreaming, thinking of opposite sex, etc.), initial inclination is to go back to work; writing little note "Get back to work" prevents this for a moment and serves to make concentration more desirable, discriminations more complete.

5. *Timer*

When timer rang students stood up immediately, took timer, and moved away from study area. Reset timer for two minutes, then engaged in "fun" activity until timer again sounded; whereupon students went through same routine filling in new card. This procedure repeated until total time period allotted for study passed. Students changed from six-minute study session to nine-minute study session when number of distraction marks (and corresponding self-written work instructions) numbered three or fewer.

6. *Study schedules*

Students permitted three-minute break for nine-minute study period. Each time distractors reduced to two or below, students moved up scale (study six, break two; study nine, break three; study twelve, break four; study fifteen, break five; study eighteen, break six; study twenty-one, break seven; study twenty-four, break eight; study twenty-seven, break nine; study thirty, break ten; study thirty-three, break eleven; study thirty-six, break twelve; study thirty-nine, break thirteen; study forty-two, break fourteen; study forty-five, break fifteen) until reaching maximum. Students were strongly encouraged to never study longer than forty-five minutes while using fifteen-minute break for pleasant activities. This routine builds strong study skills as well as gives approval rewards following each small study session.

7. *External rewards*

Some parents/students used extra incentives (movies, car privileges, staying out time, money, family outings) for moving up study scale *while maintaining absolute honesty*. Of course, many students were delighted with a routine which didn't start with amount of homework to be finished but with amount of time to be studied (when no homework available or required, student reviewed materials for test).

Evaluate: Average grades (thirty-one students) increased to B within three school terms. Follow-up indicated twenty-four students maintained this level or above during entire following school year. Five students who did *not* improve admitted to never getting with the program. Seven students who did not *maintain* grade level did not consistently adhere to program primarily as result of *parents* who did not change their normally punitive, nagging reaction; expressed doubts as to mental capabilities of their children or effectiveness of program; and who did not encourage positively through words and extra incentives. Five students with parents falling into above category succeeded in spite of parental negativism and lack of support. (All later confided to school personnel they were going to prove to parents they were not "stupid" and continued program in spite of lack of support. Three of these finally set up study places in friend's or relative's homes away from "distracting" influence of negative parents.)

Note: This routine has been used successfully with Junior High students, upper-level grade school students, college students, and professionals who need to learn discrimination between "on-task" study as opposed to clutter. Most students do not enjoy their rest or fun times because they begin to feel "guilty" about not doing work. Alternately, when they attempt to study, they begin to feel sorry for themselves because they are not out having a good time!

Professional Application

Example 111

Pinpoint: *On-task versus cluttered communication.*
(13-, 15-, and 17-year-old teen-agers, adults)

Record: "Lack of communication" reported by teen-agers and parents after initial misunderstandings regarding use of car, hour of return from dates, work responsibilities at home, school work. Discussions characterized by noise, interruptions, TV, telephone, loud talking, etc. (eighty occurrences in three two-hour periods).

Consequate: Family communication sessions instituted with rules: (1) we speak softly, (2) we speak one at a time, (3) we listen carefully, (4) we do not contradict, (5) we might have to *agree to disagree* on some issues, and (6) we will verbalize opposite viewpoint to satisfaction of other person to prove we understand. Sessions free from any extrinsic interruptions, set up daily after dinner beginning with five minutes (oven timer set) and gradually increasing to twenty minutes.

Evaluate: "On-task" communication. No interruptions during communication times; other problems decreased.

Note: Parents found this routine so successful that they instituted a time for just Mother and Dad to sit down over coffee a half-hour daily for on-task communication. Some people are seemingly afraid of this intense interaction and "inadvertently structure" their lives with so much clutter so as to avoid any sincere reciprocity. Many times people even state excuses as to why they can not do it. On-task communication is possible in almost every case; however, it must be structured.

It is unfortunate that most families do not have the opportunities to have themselves observed by an independent outside observer from the time they are together in the evening until just before bedtime. Most families have very few set routines, and not only are family members rarely giving undivided attention, but it becomes exceedingly difficult to even imagine what is supposed to be going on. When confronted with observations from their homes, many parents will reply that they value "flexibility." This begs the question.

As parents, it is important to help our children (perhaps even ourselves) to make some basic discriminations. On-task communication, for example, does not automatically occur just because two people are in proximity to one another. Time must be scheduled which ideally has no interruptions. On-task communication does not occur in movie houses, while watching television, or necessarily even when the families take some time off and spend a weekend or longer vacation together.

While worthwhile activities should be given the time and attention deserved, on-task communication should not be confused with other activities. The classic example is the father who wondered why he couldn't communicate with his son after eight years of weekend fishing together. This kind of situation might be ridiculous if results were not often so pathetic. Many parents, as well as older children, actually believe that going to the movies together, camping together, attending school functions, going to church together, etc., are prerequisites for, or somehow take the place of, communication and other important interactions. The boy in the above example could fish very well.

Parents should realize that it is specifically a cause-and-effect world. If families go to the movies together, or concerts, or football games, or any number of other activities, they learn those behaviors very well, but in almost every instance the very fact they are engaging in an activity which is demanding on-task concentration will, by necessity, limit, if not completely obliterate, the possibility for involved on-task communications. Certainly activities may give an impetus to start communication, but human beings are not able to be on-task to two things at precisely the same time and do justice to both. When families enjoy activities, they should by all means participate, but should not confuse the emotional involvement of "feeling good" while engaged in the activity with other important behaviors (communication). There are individuals who appear to never engage in any family activities, yet are on-task in time spent communicating, teaching kindness, and maintaining extremely satisfying lives with spouses and children.

Professional Application

Do I understand the examples?

Pinpoint:	*Dishonesty.* (any classroom, anywhere)
Record:	Three students caught cheating on first examination of term.
Consequate:	F grades assigned without explanation.
Evaluate:	Same three students caught stealing "ditto master" of second examination from typist's wastebasket.
Consequate II:	Each student asked to write short theme stating reasons for cheating.
Evaluate II:	Same three students caught cheating in falsifying laboratory manual.
Consequate III:	Students asked to prepare confessional speech to be delivered before entire class. Parents of two students strongly objected, stating such treatment "would not only be a terrible experience, but would damage children's reputations." Principal received call from school board member, after which students, parents, and teachers instructed to meet in principal's office. At meeting, all students denied any cheating whatsoever. Teacher presented first themes of confession. Parents of one student immediately placed her in private school. Parents of second student persuaded principal to allow their daughter to withdraw from the course. Parents of third student did not come to the meeting. Teacher required this girl to make confessional statement before class. She did, but she broke down crying before finishing. She later told teacher it was the worst thing she ever did in her life. Much

later she told teacher it was the *second* worst thing she ever did in her life.

Evaluate IV, V, VI, VII, etc.:

The science of behavior is predictable. You know all three of these students, regardless of age, sex, or position.

Do I understand?

Fictional Application

part **3**

A POSITIVE APPROACH

chapter **7**

RESPONDING
THE ART OF LOVING

Why develop responses?

Mother has prepared supper and expects her seventeen-year-old son home at approximately 6:00 P.M. Six arrives, no son; the woman begins to pace a little and thinks about a ruined supper. At 6:30 she becomes a little angry and makes statements about her inconsiderate offspring. Seven P.M. arrives, and, in spite of trying to do something else, she begins to worry about his whereabouts. Between 7:30 and 8:00 (while the rest of the family eats a cold dinner) he is imagined drowned, dead in a car wreck, attacked by muggers, unconscious in the hospital, picked up by the police, drunk in an alley, and sundry other things, all of which are negative (she has lost her appetite). Is it not strange that during these times most people don't imagine that the son happened to get involved with a classmate and forgot the time while having a wonderful talk, enjoying a pleasant stroll, meditating by oneself while looking at flowers in the park, or perhaps shopping for a surprise gift for this mother.

What, in reality, is the problem in this case?—the mother who is "fretting and worrying" about possible catastrophic events, or a seventeen-year-old son who is two hours later than usual. The real problem is the *worry*. When dinner time arrived if the mother had begun dinner, played a game with the younger children, got them ready for bed, talked to her family for a few uninterrupted minutes, and/or found an interesting book or TV program, there would be no problem.

Unfortunately, it happens frequently that many parents and families reinforce in themselves (substitute husband for son and reread the above example) and others the very worst. We train our families to worry unnecessarily about terrible things that might happen in the future, potential loss of loved ones, inability of children to succeed in the future, etc. The problem is actually the worry itself, especially when nothing is done to change behavior. Parents manage to systematically increase their worrying and, in addition, convince themselves that it is being done because of sincere concern for themselves and others.

It would seem that parents and children certainly should be trained to explicitly prepare for forseeable emergencies (what do you do when a stranger tries to pick you up? if the house is on fire and smoke is coming from the kitchen? if you break a leg? if you are offered narcotics? etc). Forseeable and even remote situations may be handled by these procedures with extensive role-playing to clarify just what should be done in emergencies. If worry occurs after these preparations, then this worry seems to be definitely not conducive to familial happiness. When we are waiting up at night for an errant progeny it is too late to do any teaching, and if some accident has occurred there is nothing to be done until we are notified.

Worry, or as commonly stated "depression" usually represents nothing more than statements to oneself or others indicating that we "feel sorry for ourself." Frequently as we interact with friends, relatives, or family and begin to spill our tale of "worry and woe," the "significant other" listens intently, nods his head, exhibits a "sad" face, and asks questions. Generally, as they perform us this disservice, we pretend they "understand" and therefore reinforce our "depression." In this situation parents might tell friends, each other, and especially their children that if one wants to feel sorry for oneself and waste precious time instead of *deciding* what to do and then working on the problem, one had better find someone who wants to be a "human garbage collector" instead of a helper. Often those who "forget" or refuse responsibilities just want to spend time complaining. If this seems to be the case (i.e., it has happened many times before) then the only negative comments we might allow are comments which honestly report the facts of a situation and are followed by an attempt to give a statement about what behaviors are being planned to alleviate the problem. "Tell me what you intend to do about it; do not give me your problem." It is astounding to find how fast "depression" and "worry" are relieved in children when no one pays attention, and the child's negative verbal behavior is either punished or ignored while positive solutions are praised. "Is that what you will do next time; that's excellent; let's pretend that I'm the other person and you show me what you will do," etc.

Also a parent should be careful not to reinforce children for crying following refusals and therefore reinforce the self-fulfilling prophecy that if only one could cry it out of his system, then he would feel better. The parent should help the child focus on delineating the problem without reinforcing emotional responses and, at the same time, take the responsibility to plan a program with the child which will lead to behaviors incompatible with feeling sorry for oneself.

Worry, anger, and other responses are expected in humans of all ages. They should be acknowledged immediately followed by behavioral techniques to change the emotion not reinforced or worried about. Children should be trained to deal with a problem immediately, rather than receive reinforcement for extended periods of worry. Hence, the focus becomes one of solving the problems which have produced the worry, anger, or crying and thus to act one's way into a new way of thinking. **Why develop responses?—To stop worrying and start acting.**

Approval responses?

The parent has many responses that may be used contingently, across time, to teach desired behaviors. However, merely reading, talking, and thinking about consequential responses does not produce optimum results. The development of effective responses takes *practice*. Consider for a moment the tremendous practice it takes for a poet to choose the precise word, for a musician to turn a beautiful phrase, for an actor to deliver an effective line. Practice in developing responses cannot be overemphasized. Just talking to yourself while looking into a mirror is very effective. A tape recorder can also be valuable in developing response skills. At first you will notice some tension—you will feel awkward and perhaps a little silly. Nevertheless, practice. A good place to start is with the words "thank you." Practice saying "thank you" with as many inflections as possible—from extreme sarcasm to sincere appreciation.

If one desires to express a sincere feeling, one must make sure the real intent will be expressed. Warm and sensitive people have developed great skill in expression. Most often, expressions are not overtly practiced; yet we all, having been often misunderstood, should be sure to communicate our thoughts and feelings most effectively. Considering all the time we spend in front of the mirror on physical appearances, is it not incongruous we do not use some of this time to develop effective personal responses? After patient practice in role-playing, you will begin to notice exciting new skill in the development of responses. Sometimes you may choose to practice with your spouse or another person who desires to be helpful in giving appropriate feedback.

Responses available to the parent may be classified in five categories: (1) words —spoken, written, (2) physical expressions—facial, bodily, (3) closeness—nearness, touching, (4) activities—social, individual, and (5) things—materials, food, playthings, awards, money. The following lists have been developed as possible *approval* models for the parent. Parents should select and develop those reinforcers deemed usable as specific behavioral contingencies. Start with one or two responses, develop them thoroughly, and evaluate them in relationship to the problem behavior before developing others.

Words Spoken: Approval

Words

Yes	Uh-huh
Good	Positively!
Nice	Go ahead
O.K.	Yeah!
Great	All right
Fascinating	Nifty
Charming	Exactly
Commendable	Cool
Delightful	Wonderful
Brilliant	Of course!
Fine	Perfect

That's clever
Correct
Excellent
Absolutely right
Keep going
How beautiful
Wonderful job!
Fantastic!
Terrific!
Swell
Beautiful job
Marvelous!

Exciting!
Pleasant
Fabulous!
Splendid
Well-mannered
Thinking
Likeable
Outstanding
That's right
Satisfactory
I'm pleased
Thank you

Sentences

I'm glad you're here.
That's a *prize* of a job.
You make me happy.
That shows thought.
I think a lot of you.
That's good work.
Remarkably well done.
You're very pleasant.
That shows a great deal of work.
That's an excellent goal.
Yes, I think you should continue.
That's better.
I like the way you explained it.
You are very sincere.
That's so good.
That's a nice face.
It is a pleasure having you with me.
That's interesting.
You make being your mother really fun.
That's sweet of you.
Well thought out.
Show us how.
You're doing better.
You are improving.
You're doing fine.
You do it very well.
That's very good.
I'm so proud of you.
I like that.
This is the best yet.

Relationships

Nice things happen to nice children.
That is very imaginative.
You are worthy of my love.
That will be of great benefit to our family.
I admire it when you act like that.
That is original thought.
I appreciate your attention.
You've been a fine credit to your family.
We are proud of your achievement.
That was very kind of you.
You catch on very quickly.
Obedience makes me happy.
That deserves my respect.
You demonstrate fine ability.
That is clear thinking.
You should be very proud of this.
That was nice of you to lend her your _____.
Show me how you got such a nice _____.
I like that—I didn't know it could be done that way.
Permission granted.
That's a good job—your brother can look up to you.
Let's watch him do it.
He accepts responsibility.
That *was* a good choice.
Show this to your father.
I know how you feel—should we continue?
I'm happy your clothes are in order.
Why don't you show your father how you got the answer?
That's a good point to bring up.
I agree.
Let's put this somewhere special.
I'd like this in my own room.
My, you have a nice attitude.
Now you're really trying.
Keep working hard, _____(name)_____.
You've improved.
Your room appears so neat.
You're a good person.
If at first you don't succeed, try, try again.
Thinking.

Words Written: Approval

Symbols

Bravo!	Good work
Improvement	Correct
Fine	Good
+	Neato
Very good	Nicely done
O.K.	Very concise
Complete	*
Enjoyable	×
Excellent	Thoughtful
Outstanding	100%
Superior	Very colorful
Perceptive	Congratulations
Well done	Yeh
Great	Show this to your dad
Wow!	For special display
Rubber stamps	A-1
Colored pencil markings	

Rules

In formulating rules, remember to:

1. Involve the child in making up the rules.
2. Keep the rules short and to the point.
3. Phrase rules where possible in a positive way. ("Sit quietly while eating," instead of "Don't talk and jump around at the table.")
4. Remind the child of the rules at times *other* than when he has misbehaved.
5. Make different sets of rules for varied activities.
6. Let children know when different rules apply (work-play).
7. Post rules in a conspicuous place and review regularly.
8. Keep the general form or notebook and record the number of times you review rules with the child.

Expressions: Approval

Facial

Looking
Smiling
Winking
Nodding
Grinning
Raising eyebrows
Forming kiss
Opening eyes
Slowly closing eyes
Laughing (happy)
Chuckling

Widening eyes
Wrinkling nose
Blinking rapidly
Giggling
Whistling
Cheering
Licking lips
Smacking lips
Pressing lips affirmatively
Rolling eyes enthusiastically

Bodily

Clapping hands
Raising arms
Shaking fist
Signaling O.K.
Jumping up and down
Cocking head
Skipping
Rubbing stomach
Thumbs up
Shaking head
Hugging self
Grabbing
Bouncing
Dancing

Stroking motions
Shrugging shoulders
Opening hands
Flipping head
Taking a fast breath
Expansive movements of hands
Covering head slowly, quickly
Patting with hands
Circling hand through air (encouragement to continue)
Hand/finger to face, eyebrows, eyes, nose, ears, mouth, cheek, lips, hair, forehead

Closeness: Approval

Nearness

Nearness concerns physical proximity and ranges from geographical separation—through noticeable contact—to embracing.

Interacting with child at playtime
Eating next to the child
Sitting on bed near child

Sitting within young child's group
Standing alongside
Lying down with child before bedtime
Gently guiding
Pausing (while transferring objects)

Touching

Hand on hand
Ruffling hair
Touching head
Patting head
Pinching cheek
Pinching chin
Touching nose
Patting back
Patting shoulder
Touching arm
Straightening clothes
Hugging
Touching hand
Shaking hands
Squeezing hand
Patting cheek
Nudging
Helping put on coats
Retying sashes

Walking alongside
Combing hair
Tying shoes
Quick squeeze
Slugging (teen-ager)
Dancing
Rubbing back of neck
Gently raising chin
Leaning over
Touching hurt
Kissing a hurt
Putting face next to child
Tweaking nose
Tickling
Cupping face in hands
Gentle pull at hair
Running finger down person's nose
Guiding with hand

Activities and Privileges: Approval

Individual

Leading family groups
Displaying child's creative work or award
Straightening up for your mother
Putting away materials
Running errands
Caring for special pets, flowers, etc.
Collecting materials (papers, workbooks, assignments, etc.)
Choosing activities
Sharing a story
Constructing toy materials
Dusting, cleaning, arranging furniture, etc.

Helping other children (drinking, lavatory, cleaning, etc.)
Reading a story
Exempting a duty
Working problems out with you
Answering questions
Outside play supervising
Leading family discussions
Making gifts
Recognizing birthdays
Writing letters
Responsibility for on-going activities (pets, plants, room)
Decorating room
Presenting hobby to rest of family

Social

Movies
Clubs
Teams
Musical groups

Things: Approval

Materials

Books—appropriate level
Pets
Bookcovers
Book markers
Coloring books
Crayons
Paints
Pencils with names
Chalk
Flowers
Buttons
Pins
Pictures
Colored paper
Pets
Counting beads
Games
Stuffed animals

Cards
Stars
Chips
Kites
Balloons
Jacks
Striped straws
Windmills
Miniature animals
Farm set and farm animals
Plastic toys (Indians, animals, soldiers, etc.)
Jump ropes
Musical toys
Wind-up toys
Hand puppets
Marbles
Building blocks

Lego

See N' Say toys

Lincoln Logs

Beads

Gum ball machine

Balls

Sand toys (bucket, shovel, etc.)

Play money

Banks

Peg board and peg towns

Telephones

Silly Sand

Silly Putty

Play Dough

Pick-up sticks

Blocks

Jack 'n box

Bath toys (boats, rubber ducks, etc.)

Pounding blocks

Doctor kits

Nurse kits

Tops

Tool bench and tools

Tinker toys

Fire engine

Yo-yo

Boats

Trains & equipment

Bean bags

Cars and gas stations

Racing cars

Trucks

Tractors

Steam shovels

Dolls and equipment (bottles, clothes, etc.)

Doll houses

Doll furniture

Talking dolls

Buggies

Kaleidoscopes

Flashlight

Strollers

Kitchen equipment (play stove, sink, refrigerator)

Comic books

Food mixes

Utensil sets

Household items (pots, coffee can, paper rolls, cardboard boxes, etc.)

Dishes

Money (exchangeable, token)

Stamps

Cleaning sets (carpet sweepers, brooms, etc.)

Play furniture (table, chairs, etc.)

Purses

Umbrellas

Costumes

Jumping beans

Ice cream maker

Popcorn maker

Cotton candy maker

Cash register

Switch board

Electric football, baseball, basketball, hockey

Cowboy dolls and equipment

Knights, castles, and equipment

Model kits (cars, planes, ships, etc.)

Pinball machine

Bicycle

Tricycle

Music boxes

Rocking horse

Bird houses

Ant houses

Bug houses

Suit cases

Wall decorations

Nicknacks

Sewing machine

Sewing boxes

Typewriters

Playing cards

Record player

Walkie-talkie

Records
Stationery
Calendars
Musical instruments
Bulletin boards
Desk organizers (notes, books, pencils, etc.)
Cameras and equipment
Photo album
Label maker
Pencil sharpener
Stapler
Autograph book
Date book
Address books
Pencils
Pens
Radios
Tape recorders
Watches
Vanity sets
Jewelry
Masks and wax disguises
Perfume
Bath powder
Bath oil
Bubble bath
Hats and clothes
Make up
Hair ribbons
Hair bands
Hair barrels
Hairdryers
Belts
Jewelry boxes
Puzzles (jigsaw, trauma tower, dice cube, wooden cube, solitaire, pyramid, mad maze, three dimensional, etc.)
Collections (coins, rocks, glass, leaves, stamps, etc.)
World globe
View master
Telescope

Microscope
Erector set
Trains
Science kits
  Frog dissecting kit
  Chemistry set
  Slide preparing kit
  Geologist's kit
  Biological kit
  Radio kit
  Computer kit
  Electric builder kit
  Rock identification kit
  Magnetic kits
  Body kits (man, woman, heart, head, skeleton, eye, ear, etc.)
Creative craft kits
  Origami (paperfolding)
  Wood burning
  Hand bag decorating
  Embroidery
  Decoupage
  Wall decorations
  Marquetry
  Mosaics
  Pillow
  Clay
  Yarn
  Ceramics
  Beads
  Leather
  Colored pipe cleaners
  Cloth
  Rock polishing
  Papier maché
  Wood
  Felt
  Tile
  Glass
  Paper
Art sets
  Oils
  Watercolors
  Pastels

Chalk
Colored pencils
Bowling equipment (ball, shoes, etc.)
Swimming equipment (fins, face mask, etc.)
Kickball
Golf equipment (clubs, balls, etc.)
Ping pong equipment
Pool table
Football equipment
Baseball equipment
Tennis equipment
Skiing equipment
Ice skates
Roller skates
Scuba diving equipment
Sleigh
Toboggan

Swing
Swing sets
Slide
Boxing gloves
Striking bag
Body building equipment
Horse shoe set
Croquet set
Badminton set
Tackraw
Darts
Tether ball
Camping equipment (sleeping bag, lantern, stove, etc.)
Fishing equipment (rod, reel, etc.)
Pets
Money
Books—appropriate level

Food

Jaw breakers
Chocolate creams
Cake
Lemonade
Popcorn
Peanuts
Ice cream
Cookies
Sugar-coated cereals
Apples
Crackers
Raisins
Candy kisses
Fruit
Crackers
Life savers

Lemon drops
Sugar cane
Candied apples
Candy canes
Candy corn
Animal crackers
Soft drinks
Milk
Marshmallows
Gum
Juices
Lollipops
Popsicles
Candy bars
Potato chips

Approval responses—What is the alternative?

Disapproval responses?

The following lists contain *disapproval* responses. The parent should study these lists carefully in order to achieve two important discriminations: (1) To recognize responses one may be unwittingly using and wish to eliminate or replace with incompatible approval responses, and (2) to plan carefully, responsibly, and cautiously the application of disapproval. The authors believe most of the following should *never* be used. *The parent must discriminate.* Even a pleasant hello can be a scathing indictment if the tone and intensity of the voice causes that effect.

Words Spoken: Disapproval

This list includes naggings, sarcasms, bitternesses, dishonesties, and other ineffectual responses whose angry delivery generally demonstrates that the *parent,* not the child, has the problem.

Impractical.
Be prompt.
Work faster.
Try to understand.
Do your homework.
Do your best.
Unclear explanation.
Don't you want to do things right?
It can't be that difficult.
You're too slow.
Stop talking.
Behave.
Pay attention.
Don't.
Wrong.
Stupid.
Be still.
Follow directions.
Think for a change.
Use some thought.
No, that's not what I said.
Would you like to get spanked?
You don't understand because you don't listen!
Be quiet and sit down.
You're gutless.
That's ridiculous.

Meaningless.
Absurd.
Bad.
Nonsense.
Too vague.
Try harder.
Wrong.
That's not right.
Incorrect.
Unsatisfactory.
Poor.
Undesirable.
You should be ashamed.
Useless.
That's not clear.
I dislike that.
Don't be silly.
That's terrible.
What is this?
Is this something?
Quit making messes.
Let's throw this away.
That's not mature.
I can't understand anything you do.
Haven't you learned how to do it yet?
Grow up!
You're not doing as well as you have done.
Horrible.
Absolutely not!
Shh!
Stop.
Listen to me.
Maddening.
Be quiet.
Stop that laughing.
I'll have no more from you.
Apologize now.
Sloppy.
Shut up!
I'll show you who's boss.
One more time and you'll get it!
Finish it now.
No talking.
I'll slap you silly.

Look for your clothes.
Leave her alone.
You march straight to your room.
You lack interest and motivation.
I'll give you something to cry about.
You *couldn't* have done it worse.
I do not like this.
I will not repeat it.
I'm not telling you again.
You're dull.
That's ugly.
You idiot.
You're a laughingstock.
It's hopeless for you.
Why are you such a "fraidy cat"?
That's cheap.
You're worthless.
You're rude.
Don't be crabby with me.
You're disgusting.
You little monster.
Don't laugh at me.
Cut it out.
You're dumb.
You're filthy.
You naughty boy.
Mock me and you won't hear the end of it.
That's narrow-minded.
That's childish.
Simple Simon.
No! No!! No!!!
You haven't applied yourself at all.
That work isn't acceptable.
What do you mean you're not finished?
Stand up straight when you talk to me.
Just try that once more.
Anyone else!
Learn that!
You'd better get on the stick.
So you're doing it again!
Speak when you're spoken to!
Smart Alec.
You *must* be confused.
I don't see your point.

You know what happened the last time you did that.
You do this work over right now.
You know better than that.
Play fair.
Don't cause problems.
You're never dependable.
That wasn't the right thing to do.
Well, we'll never do this again.
If you had a brain in your head, you wouldn't say that.
Do it!
You think you're the only one here?
You're bad.
Poor stupid oaf.
Wrong again.
You're doomed to failure.
You're wrong all the time.
You don't know anything.
You make me sick.
You're just an inadequate person.
Impertinent _____.
You're not thinking.
You haven't been paying attention.
Wipe that silly grin off your face.
I guess I shouldn't expect any more from *you*.
You're just plain boring.
You have a dirty mind.
Terrible! Terrible!
This isn't what *I* had in mind.
You know that's wrong.
Stupid nonsense.
You'd *better* try harder.
People never change.

Expressions: Disapproval

Frowning	Furrowing brows
Staring	Wrinkling nose
Curling lip	Smirking
Wrinkling forehead	Pounding fists on table
Lifting eyebrows	Lowering eyebrows
Nose in air	Laughing
Looking at ceiling	Shaking finger or fist
Puckering lips	Shaking head

Wrinkling mouth
Turning away
Squinting eyes
Gritting teeth
Biting lips
Twisting side of mouth
Squinting eyebrows
Cackling
Looking sideways
Snickering
Closing eyes
Turning head away
Clicking tongue
Letting out breath

Pushing mouth to one side
Raising lips
Pointing finger
Hissing
Putting hand behind ear
Fingers in front of lips
Grimacing
Nodding head (no)
Sniffing
Showing teeth
Tightening jaw
Pulling in bottom lip
Sticking out tongue

Closeness: Disapproval

Closeness disapproval concerns corporal punishment and ranges from threatening approaches—through spanking—to severe physical beatings.

Activities and Privileges: Disapproval

Disapproval concerning activities and privileges constitutes various degrees of *deprivation*. Deprivation ranges from withholding of privileges—through isolation—to social incarceration.

Isolation (time-out)
Ostracism
Silence periods
Sitting in corner
Staying after meals
Eating alone
Pointing out bad examples
Writing letters of apology

Writing misbehaviors
Leaving family room
Extra work
Staying in from play
Being last to leave
Away from friends
Apologizing to neighbors
Doing extra work

Things: Disapproval

Concerning things, disapproval refers to inanimate materials that are damaging to the body: (1) intense noises (ear damage), (2) heat (fires and stoves, (3) chemical (poisons), and (4) objects in motion (knives, cars, bullets, radiation). Obviously *none* of these should ever be used by the parent.

Parent/child interactions should be exciting and satisfying for both parent and child. The ingenious parent has too many positive and effective resources available to resort to shoddy and punitive measures. Many older parents state that almost all their earlier punitive consequences could have been handled in a more positive manner. A parent who truly cares will practice developing *positive* responses.

Disapproval responses?—What is the alternative?

The final goal?

It is clear that the final goal of parenthood is to provide the child with behaviors necessary for self-discipline. Indeed, persons whom we as parents have the privilege to instruct and teach at some point in time must be able to be independent. This is, perhaps, the end for which the beginning was made. The goal is achieved less often than most parents would desire. Our children sometimes leave in anger, because of age, to find a job, gain an education, go to war, but generally not because they have developed sufficient "love" for themselves and others to achieve a state of "independence." We hope that when they must leave for other reasons that then they will be independent. It behooves us to insure that this important goal is achieved for when other conditions impinge upon the child's environment he must be prepared.

When an individual has learned from his past reinforcement history to hierarchically arrange his values, when he is able to work productively over long periods of time, when he is able to delay gratification, when he is able to be content with his own company and refrain from haphazardly seeking out other individuals, when he is able to modify and control the environment that, in turn, controls him, then perhaps he has achieved an appropriate level of independence. Many problems arise in family relationships because one or more of the family members sometimes including parents are unable to exhibit any independent behavior. Additionally, some parents are concerned with vague concepts of "togetherness" that somehow are supposed to develop positive values automatically. Like many ideas (as opposed to overt behaviors) these concepts are highly elusive. When parents sincerely believe that children will turn out all right if only the family spends enough time together, this may be devastating.

It is necessary to specify both the specific behaviors that the individuals value in terms of "independence," as well as the precise amount of time necessary to effect common family goals (e.g., honesty, kindness, communication, common pursuits, family play time, etc.). Before structuring training for independence, parents should (1) assess specific values that they cherish and arrange these values in a hierarchical order from the most to the least important, (2) define specific behaviors which relate to each of the abstract values, and then (3) teach these values following the behavioral model. The amount of time to be devoted to teaching as well as the time important to spend with certain individuals (alone or in family groups) should be outlined.

"Independence," or lack of it, becomes a problem when individuals are unable to be happy when alone or sometimes even when with others. It would seem that everyone should learn to be happy under each condition as both situations are considered important. Therefore, structuring specified temporal intervals is important. Family members should be helped with programs which increase both independent activity and joint activity. The truly happy families seem to be those where it is possible for each individual to be happy alone, perhaps even for extended periods of time when necessary (military service, etc.) and also very happy when together. This condition is not accomplished by children becoming dependent upon others to provide a little more life into an otherwise dull existence. Regular programs to occupy the mind can be developed in advance and be readily available when a person begins to think about how lonely he is or wishes that someone else were there.

Some families value extensive home life and choose to spend a great deal of time together. However, when families choose to be apart (work, projects, absences for vacations) or are forced to be apart (military service), the most nonproductive activity in which a person can engage is wishing the other person were there to relieve the misery or boredom. Each family member can develop in himself and reinforce in others independent activities as well as thoughts so as not to be miserable when absence occurs. You never do a person a favor by letting him get away with something he doesn't like in himself. **The final goal—Independence.**

SUMMARY

Loving—the art of discipline

Many parents lose the love of their children because they have not developed effective techniques of behavioral control and response consistency. While some parents believe that discipline refers to a continuum from permissiveness through strictness, it is easily observed that this is not the case. Effective discipline ensues from direct cause-and-effect relationships. Therefore, concepts such as spanking versus loving, freedom versus dictatorship, expression versus subjugation are extremely deceptive. Indeed, *we only discipline those we love;* social freedom can only exist within defined limits; and self-expression, much like everything else, must be learned. *The reason we discipline is to provide each child with behaviors necessary for individual productivity and happiness.* Realizing that decisions determining what constitutes these basic behaviors are our responsibility, we should structure wisely and not deceive ourselves by stating that children are deciding all things for themselves. When we teach children to think (i.e., establish values, decide), we should do so with the express purpose of insuring logical sequencing and not use the euphemism "thinking" as a rationalization to eschew the responsibility of our job. Every parent should initially realize that the parent's primary responsibility is to assist in the child's acculturation and future independence. Teaching a child to read, write, or to be well-behaved represents the imposition of social and parental values which do not originate with the child. The parent who states, "Oh, but that's not what I mean" obviously needs some personal remediation in thought processes to differentiate between those aspects of life which are definitely mutually exclusive and those which ar not. Every parent should know precisely what decisions are to be the child's and what decisions are to be the parent's. If a parent accepts this responsibility and does not try to "give the problem away," children will acquire the basic learning necessary to develop their own values. *Regardless, one should realize that it takes a tremendous amount of courage to act on the basis of one's value orientation, parent or child.*

Discipline—the way to learning

The first aspect of discipline both socially and regarding work-tasks is to determine just *where the child is.* This is, to determine what behaviors currently are present and, therefore, know precisely where to start. Regarding school work this involves structuring the subject in easily attainable sequential steps beginning at the child's own level. In assessing inappropriate social responses the deviant behavior itself is the foremost concern. *An involved history of how the child got that way is both unproductive and unnecessary.* Academic assessments should take several days; social assessment, several minutes. All too often knowledge concerning a child's terrible adjustment, bizarre past experiences, or personality test scores provide the opportunity for some parents to give up on the child because they discover a "reason" for the inappropriate behavior. *The responsibility for discipline resides with parents.* If children are not "motivated to be well-behaved," then motivation must be taught before the parent should expect it to be internalized; it must come from without before it can be from within. *Desire for learning* (motivation) *is taught by establishing rewards for correct learning responses,* first extrinsically, later intrinsically. Realizing that at some point *learning usually represents work,* the parent must stretch the ratio of previously established rewards to motivate children through the difficult times. This represents a process of partial reinforcement to teach for long-term goals, i.e., to establish maturity.

Learning—the modification of behavior

Learning necessitates experience, discrimination, and association. *Behavior modification is a process for structuring learning experiences to provide fine discriminations and correct associations.* However, parents must deal with specified overtly demonstrable behaviors if they expect to know if desirable behaviors have been learned. It has been demonstrated that if a child knows precisely what is expected of him, and he wants to do it, he probably will. *Since inappropriate as well as appropriate behavior is learned,* preparing expectancies for children necessitates the structure of goals. Structuring goals usually represents at least to some degree parents' imposition of their value system and, therefore, it is they who *decide who decides.*

If incorrect associations have been learned, then parents must also decide *who has the problem* to keep from being confused or perhaps even irresponsible concerning what to do to change the child's behavior. The parents' structured goals should represent definable overt responses which are realistic, manageable, and above all measurable. All behaviors, both appropriate and inappropriate must be classified accurately and pinpointed in regard to the responsibility of all concerned.

Behavior—the contingent result of life

Behaviors are learned in time through contingent reinforcement. Indeed, behavior is a result of its consequences. Therefore, the parent must structure the child's life experiences if effective learning and productive living is to take place. How much control is to be exercised depends upon the values of the parents. *Reinforcement learning requires the structure of approval and disapproval responses, across time, to shape desired behavior toward specific goals. Deviant behavior is often eliminated by cutting out the payoff; wholesome learning is established by instituting a payoff.* To become proficient in behavioral analysis, the parent must observe the child closely, paying particular attention to what happens immediately before and after a specified behavior to ascertain what constitutes reward. It should be remembered that when the parent begins to structure or restructure for the child, problems of "fairness" arise. Parents then must discriminate between many separate and related issues to decide what is to be done, i.e., *what's fair.* Approval-disapproval reinforcers that may be used contingently include every available personal response as well as all objects at parents' disposal: words, expressions, closeness, activities, and things. *These contingencies must be structured if effective learning is to take place.* Just thinking about responses is not enough to develop these tools effectively.

Life—the structure of activities in time

Everything happens in time, indeed, *life is time.* Temporal aspects of life are not only extremely important but highly elusive. Therefore, precise timing in delivering responses cannot be overemphasized. *While temporal consistency is the single most important aspect of discipline, it is also the most difficult.* In order to discipline effectively, the parent must structure everything across time. Structural manipulation of the external environment is based upon: (1) Pinpoint—defining the problem behavior to be eliminated, the new behavior to be learned or both (structuring for incompatible responses). Pinpointing regarding work tasks is accomplished by structuring specific measurable goals; pinpointing inappropriate social responses necessitates defining deviant responses specifically in overt categories and observing the child carefully. These observations not only establish what stimuli are presently reinforcing undesired behavior but also provide clues for selecting effective reinforcers which can then be used to establish other responses. (2) Record—assessing behavior quantitatively. It is imperative that accurate records be kept. Otherwise the parent can never ascertain the relationship between the frequency and magnitude of the old, social or work-appropriate or inappropriate, behaviors and the new. Records must be precise and recordings must be done across time in precise time intervals. (3) Consequate—controlling the child's external environment through the use of approval-disapproval reinforcers delivered contingently on time schedules to insure desired behaviors. (4) Evaluate—measuring the frequency of behavior to see if the behavior gets better or worse. *If at first you don't succeed, then new structure is required.* When parents structure contingencies the long term effects of specific reinforcers cannot be considered too carefully. *Being a good parent requires good taste in selecting appropriate responses.*

Time—the measurement of responding

As behavioral principles are practiced and applied, we become confident that wrong associations can indeed be changed. After myths are laid aside; after we stop feeling guilty, stop worrying, and start acting—the parent begins to change. Subsequently, behavior becomes more predictable and effects of specific actions assured. *Parents then realize that behavioral procedures will indeed work with their child.*

The foremost requirement of a behavioral approach, however, is that the *behavior(s) under question must be measured accurately and objectively.* Recording procedures are not difficult: one needs only paper, pencil, and some measurement of time. The General Observation Form provides an excellent way to keep accurate records. Behaviors are defined (pinpointed) and observed by simply writing down the specified behavior and then checking its occurrence during the planned recording procedure. Consequences are applied systematically (also recorded), then the behavior is again measured in order to evaluate the effect of the consequence. Most often, thoughtfully prescribed contingencies decrease objectionable behaviors from the original recorded level and/or increase desirable responses. *The many scientific and professional examples demonstrate that if selected reinforcers are not effective, a new structure may be required and other contingencies established.* Restructuring regarding all aspects of providing for the child should represent a continuous process toward greater refinement. *Increased behavioral effectiveness will demonstrate that parents do indeed understand.*

Responding—the art of loving

While worry, anger, and other responses are expected in humans of all ages, these responses should be acknowledged and immediately followed by behavioral techniques to change the person's nonproductive behavior. *The reason we develop productive responses is so that we can stop worrying and start acting.* Children should be trained to deal with a problem immediately, rather than receive reinforcement for extended periods of depression. Parents have many *approval* responses that may be developed and used contingently to teach these desired behaviors. However, merely reading, discussing, and thinking about consequential responses does not produce optimum results. The development of effective responses takes practice. As parents study *disapproval* responses they will become more sensitive to their own responding as well as challenged to plan carefully any use of disapproval. It is axiomatic that children learn what they live. Furthermore, it behooves parents to prepare a child for some situations the child has not previously experienced. Thus parents must not only provide an environment to stimulate effective teaching within the home, more importantly, *prepare the child for future independence.*

Effective reinforcing toward better child rearing takes much practice. Similar to other pursuits in life, the rewards seem both proportional to, and contingent upon, thoughtful involvement, structured action, and continuous learning and evaluation. If hopes are realized, the end product of this training will be a person who is independent, who is individually productive, socially responsible, and, above all, personally happy. A person who has the ability to analyze, criticize, and choose alternatives and who has a compelling system of values whereby he may actualize his life in a manner consistent with ever-increasing knowledge—in a word, a person who evidences *discipline*.

REFERENCES FOR
SCIENTIFIC APPLICATIONS

EXAMPLE
NUMBER

5 Russo, S. Adaptations in behavioral therapy with children. *Behavior Research and Therapy,* 1964, *2,* 43–47.

6 Doubros, S. G., and Daniels, C. J. An experimental approach to the reduction of overactive behavior. *Behavior Research and Therapy,* 1966, *4,* 251–258.

11 Becker, W. C.; Madsen, C. H., Jr.; Arnold, C. R.; and Thomas, D. R. The contingent use of teacher attention and praise in reducing classroom problems. *Journal of Special Education,* 1967, *1,* 287–307.

18 Kobasigawa, A. Inhibitory and disinhibitory effects of models on sex-appropriate behavior in children. *Psychologia,* 1968, *11,* 86–96.

19 Martin, R. R., and Siegel, G. M. The effects of response contingent shock on stuttering. *Journal of Speech and Hearing Research,* 1966, *9,* 340–352.

23 Dickinson, Changing behavior with behavioral techniques. *Journal of School Psychology,* 1968, *6,* 276–283.

24 Williams, C. D. The elimination of tantrum behavior by extinction procedures. *Journal of Abnormal and Social Psychology,* 1959, *59,* 269.

25 Madsen, C. H., Jr. Positive reinforcement in the toilet training of a normal child: a case report. In *Case Studies in Behavior Modification,* eds. L. P. Ullmann, and L. Krasner. New York: Holt, Rinehart and Winston, 1965, 305–307.

26 Kennedy, W. A. School phobia: rapid treatment of fifty cases. *Journal of Abnormal Psychology,* 1965, *70,* 285–289.

29 Tasto, D. L. Systematic desensitization, muscle relaxation, and visual imagery in the counter conditioning of a four year old boy. *Behavior Research and Therapy,* 1969, *7,* 409–411.

32 Lovaas, O. I. Control of food intake in children by reinforcement of relevant verbal behavior. *Journal of Abnormal and Social Psychology,* 1968, *68,* 672–678.

34 Peterson, D. R., and London, P. A role for cognition in the behavioral treatment of a child's eliminative disturbance. In *Case Studies in Behavior Modification,* eds. L. P. Ullmann, and L. Krasner. New York: Holt, Rinehart and Winston, 1965, 289–295.

36 Holmes, D. S. The application of learning theory to the treatment of a school behavior problem: a case study. *Psychology in the Schools,* 1966, *3,* 355–359.

EXAMPLE
NUMBER

39 Lal, H., and Lindsey, O. R. Therapy of chronic constipation in young child by social contingencies. *Behavior Research and Therapy,* 1968, *6,* 484–485.

44 Harris, F. R.; Johnston, M. K.; Kelly, C. S.; and Wolf, M. M. Effects of positive social reinforcement on regressed crawling of a nursery school child. *Journal of Educational Psychology,* 1964, *55,* 35–41.

45 Harris, F. R.; Wolf, M. M.; and Baer, D. M. Effects of adult social reinforcement of child behavior. *Young Children,* 1964, *20,* 8–17.

46 Reynolds, N. J., and Risley, T. R. The role of social and material reinforcers in increasing talking of a disadvantaged preschool child. *Journal of Applied Behavior Analysis,* 1968, *1,* 253–262.

48 Allen, K. E.; Hart, B. M.; Buell, J. S.; Harris, F. R.; and Wolf, M. M. Effects of social reinforcement on isolate behavior of a nursery school child. *Child Development,* 1964, *35,* 511–518.

50 Madsen, C. H., Jr.; Becker, W. C.; and Thomas, D. R. Rules, praise, and ignoring: elements of elementary classroom control. *Journal of Applied Behavior Analysis,* 1968, *1,* 139–150.

51 Holland, C. J. Elimination by the parents of fire setting behavior in a seven year old boy. *Behavior Research and Therapy,* 1969, *7,* 135–137.

52 O'Leary, K. D., and Becker, W. C. The effects of the intensity of a teacher's reprimands on children's behavior. *Journal of School Psychology,* 1968, *7,* 8–11.

54 Ratliff, R. G., and Stein, N. H. Treatment of neurodermatitis by behavior therapy: a case study. *Behavior Research and Therapy,* 1968, *6,* 397–399.

55 Jersild, A. T., and Holmes, F. B. Methods of overcoming children's fears. *Journal of Psychology,* 1935, *1,* 75–104.

57 O'Leary, K. D.; O'Leary, S.; and Becker, W. C. Modification of a deviant sibling interaction pattern in the home. *Behavior Research and Therapy,* 1967, *5,* 113–120.

58 Lattal, K. A. Contingency management of toothbrushing behavior in a summer camp for children. *Applied Behavior Analysis,* 1969, *2,* 195–198.

59 Bentler, P. M. An infant's phobia treated with reciprocal inhibition therapy. *Journal of Child Psychology and Psychiatry,* 1962, *3,* 185–189.

64 Miller, K. A note on the control of study behavior. *Journal of Experimental Child Psychology,* 1965, *1,* 108–110.

66 Brown, P., and Elliott, R. Control of aggression in a nursery school class. *Journal of Experimental Child Psychology,* 1965, *2,* 103–107.

67 Resnick, J. H. The control of smoking behavior by stimulus satiation. *Behavior Research and Therapy,* 1968, *6,* 397–399.

71 Schwitzgebel, R., and Kolb, D. A. Inducing behavior changes in adolescent delinquents. *Behavior Research and Therapy,* 1964, *1,* 297–304.

EXAMPLE
NUMBER

75 Zeilberger, J.; Sampson, S. E.; and Sloane, H. N., Jr. Modification of a child's problem behaviors in the home with the mother as therapist. *Journal of Applied Behavior Analysis*, 1969, *1*, 47–53.

77 Madsen, C. H., Jr.; Hoffman, M.; Thomas, D. R.; Koropsak, E.; and Madsen, C. K. Comparisons of toilet training techniques. In *Social Learning in Childhood: Readings in Theory and Application*. Belmont, California: Brooks-Cole, 1969, 124–132.

87 Madsen, C. K., and Madsen, C. H., Jr. Music as a behavior modification technique with a juvenile delinquent. *Journal of Music Therapy*, 1968, *5*, 69–76.

90 Davison, G. C. Self-control through "imaginal aversive contingency" and "one-downmanship" enabling the powerless to accommodate unreasonableness. In *Behavioral Counseling: Cases and Techniques*, eds. J. D. Krumblotz, and C. E. Thoresen. New York: Holt, Rinehart and Winston, 1969, 319–327.

95 Burgess, E. P. Elimination of vomiting behavior. *Behavior Research and Therapy*, 1969, *7*, 173–176.

101 Ellson, D. G.; Barber, L.; Engle, T. L.; and Kampwerth, L. Programmed tutoring: a teaching aid and research tool. *Reading Research Quarterly*, 1965, *1*, 77–127.

102 Conger, J. C. The treatment of encopresis by the management of social consequences. *Behavior Therapy*, 1970, *1*, 386–390.

103 Hawkins, R. P.; Peterson, R. F.; Schweid, E.; and Bijou, S. W. Behavior therapy in the home: Amelioration of problem parent-child relations with the parent in a therapeutic role. *Journal of Experimental Child Psychology*, 1966, *4*, 99–107.

106 Bailey, J. S.; Wolf, M. M.; and Phillips, E. L. Home-based reinforcement of pre-delinquents classroom behavior. *Journal of Applied Behavior Analysis*, 1970, *3*, 14–24.

109 Wahler, R. J.; Winkel, G. H.; Peterson, R. E.; and Morrison, D. C. Mothers as behavior therapists for their own children. *Behavior Research and Therapy*, 1965, *3*, 113–124.

General Observation Form

PINPOINT_____ Person(s) observed_____

Observer(s)_____ Location_____

Time of obs. _____ Desire that behavior increase decrease

I (we) will conduct _____ observations per _____ every _____ for _____
               (number)   (min-hr-day)   (day-wk)   (day-wk)

before consequating takes place.

Observation interval _____ Time between obs. _____
            (sec-min-hr-day)   (sec-min-hr-day)

RECORD Each occurrence of Pinpoint			CONSEQUATE Consequences following occurrence of behavior					EVALUATE Each occurrence of Pinpoint		
Date	Obs #		Date	Obs #	Approval	Dis-approval	Other	Date	Obs #	

Total = _____   Totals = _____   _____ _____   Total = _____

\# Obs. = _____   \# Obs. = _____

Average = _____   When _____   When_____   Average = _____

Comments _____
_____
_____
_____
_____
_____
_____

(appropriate)
for _____
   (time-times)
Then these approvals will follow:
a. _____
b. _____
c. _____

(inappropriate)
Then this disapproval will follow:
a. _____

Summary:
Record total _____
Evaluate total_____
Record average_____
Evaluate avg._____
Increase_____
Decrease _____

General Observation Form

PINPOINT _____ Person(s) observed _____

Observer(s) _____ Location _____

Time of obs. _____ Desire that behavior increase decrease

I (we) will conduct _____ observations per _____ every _____ for _____
               (number)   (min-hr-day)   (day-wk)   (day-wk)
before consequating takes place.

Observation interval _____ Time between obs. _____
               (sec-min-hr-day)   (sec-min-hr-day)

RECORD Each occurrence of Pinpoint		CONSEQUATE Consequences following occurrence of behavior					EVALUATE Each occurrence of Pinpoint		
Date	Obs #	Date	Obs #	Approval	Dis-approval	Other	Date	Obs #	

Total = _____   Totals = _____   _____ _____   Total = _____
\# Obs. = _____   \# Obs. = _____
Average = _____   When _____   When _____   Average = _____

Comments _____
_____
_____
_____
_____
_____
_____

(appropriate)
for _____
   (time-times)
Then these approvals
will follow:
a. _____
b. _____
c. _____

(inappropriate)
Then this
disapproval
will follow:
a. _____

Summary:
Record total _____
Evaluate total _____
Record average _____
Evaluate avg. _____
Increase _____
Decrease _____

General Observation Form

PINPOINT_____   Person(s) observed_____

Observer(s)_____   Location_____

Time of obs. _____   Desire that behavior increase decrease

I (we) will conduct _____ observations per _____ every _____ for _____
               (number)   (min-hr-day)   (day-wk)   (day-wk)
before consequating takes place.

Observation interval _____   Time between obs. _____
                     (sec-min-hr-day)   (sec-min-hr-day)

RECORD Each occurrence of Pinpoint			CONSEQUATE Consequences following occurrence of behavior					EVALUATE Each occurrence of Pinpoint		
Date	Obs #		Date	Obs #	Approval	Dis-approval	Other	Date	Obs #	

Total = _____   Totals = _____   _____ _____   Total = _____
\# Obs. = _____   \# Obs. = _____
Average = _____   When _____   When _____   Average = _____

Comments _____

for _____ (appropriate)

(time-times)

Then these approvals will follow:

a. _____

b. _____

c. _____

(inappropriate)

Then this disapproval will follow:

a. _____

Summary:

Record total _____

Evaluate total _____

Record average _____

Evaluate avg _____

Increase _____

Decrease _____

General Observation Form

PINPOINT _____   Person(s) observed _____

Observer(s) _____   Location _____

Time of obs. _____   Desire that behavior increase decrease

I (we) will conduct _____ observations per _____ every _____ for _____
                (number)   (min-hr-day)   (day-wk)   (day-wk)
before consequating takes place.

Observation interval _____   Time between obs. _____
             (sec-min-hr-day)   (sec-min-hr-day)

RECORD Each occurrence of Pinpoint			CONSEQUATE Consequences following occurrence of behavior					EVALUATE Each occurrence of Pinpoint		
Date	Obs #		Date	Obs #	Approval	Dis-approval	Other	Date	Obs #	

Total = _____   Totals = _____   _____ _____   Total = _____
\# Obs. = _____   \# Obs. = _____
Average = _____   When _____   When _____   Average = _____

Comments _____

(appropriate)
for _____
(time-times)
Then these approvals will follow:
a. _____
b. _____
c. _____

(inappropriate)
Then this disapproval will follow:
a. _____

Summary:
Record total _____
Evaluate total _____
Record average _____
Evaluate avg. _____
Increase _____
Decrease _____

General Observation Form

PINPOINT_____   Person(s) observed_____

Observer(s)_____   Location_____

Time of obs. _____   Desire that behavior increase decrease

I (we) will conduct _____ observations per _____ every _____ for _____
                    (number)   (min-hr-day)   (day-wk)   (day-wk)

before consequating takes place.

Observation interval _____   Time between obs. _____
                     (sec-min-hr-day)   (sec-min-hr-day)

RECORD Each occurrence of Pinpoint			CONSEQUATE Consequences following occurrence of behavior					EVALUATE Each occurrence of Pinpoint		
Date	Obs #		Date	Obs #	Approval	Dis-approval	Other	Date	Obs #	

Total = _____   Totals = _____   _____ _____   Total = _____
# Obs. = _____   # Obs. = _____
Average = _____   When _____   When _____   Average = _____

Comments _____

(appropriate)
for _____
(time-times)
Then these approvals will follow:
a. _____
b. _____
c. _____

(inappropriate)
Then this disapproval will follow:
a. _____

Summary:
Record total _____
Evaluate total _____
Record average _____
Evaluate avg. _____
Increase _____
Decrease _____

General Observation Form

PINPOINT _____ Person(s) observed _____

Observer(s) _____ Location _____

Time of obs. _____ Desire that behavior increase decrease

I (we) will conduct _____ observations per _____ every _____ for _____
              (number)   (min-hr-day)   (day-wk)   (day-wk)
before consequating takes place.

Observation interval _____ Time between obs. _____
            (sec-min-hr-day)   (sec-min-hr-day)

RECORD Each occurrence of Pinpoint			CONSEQUATE Consequences following occurrence of behavior					EVALUATE Each occurrence of Pinpoint		
Date	Obs #		Date	Obs #	Approval	Dis-approval	Other	Date	Obs #	

Total = _____   Totals = _____   _____ _____   Total = _____
\# Obs. = _____   \# Obs. = _____
Average = _____   When _____   When _____   Average = _____

Comments _____
_____
_____
_____
_____
_____
_____

for _____
   (appropriate)
  (time-times)
Then these approvals
will follow:
a. _____
b. _____
c. _____

(inappropriate)
Then this
disapproval
will follow:
a. _____

Summary:
Record total _____
Evaluate total _____
Record average _____
Evaluate avg. _____
Increase _____
Decrease _____

General Observation Form

PINPOINT _____   Person(s) observed _____

Observer(s) _____   Location _____

Time of obs. _____   Desire that behavior increase decrease

I (we) will conduct _____ observations per _____ every _____ for _____

               (number)   (min-hr-day)   (day-wk)   (day-wk)

before consequating takes place.

Observation interval _____   Time between obs. _____

               (sec-min-hr-day)   (sec-min-hr-day)

RECORD Each occurrence of Pinpoint			CONSEQUATE Consequences following occurrence of behavior					EVALUATE Each occurrence of Pinpoint		
Date	Obs #		Date	Obs #	Approval	Dis-approval	Other	Date	Obs #	

Total = _____   Totals = _____   _____ _____   Total = _____

\# Obs. = _____   \# Obs. = _____

Average = _____   When _____   When _____   Average = _____

Comments _____

(appropriate)   (inappropriate)   Summary:

for _____   Then this   Record total _____

(time-times)   disapproval   Evaluate total _____

Then these approvals   will follow: Record average _____

will follow: a. _____   Evaluate avg. _____

a. _____   Increase _____

b. _____   Decrease _____

c. _____

General Observation Form

PINPOINT_____ Person(s) observed_____

Observer(s)_____ Location_____

Time of obs. _____ Desire that behavior increase decrease

I (we) will conduct _____ observations per _____ every _____ for _____

\qquad\qquad (number) \qquad\qquad\qquad (min-hr-day) \qquad (day-wk) \qquad (day-wk)

before consequating takes place.

Observation interval _____ Time between obs. _____

\qquad\qquad (sec-min-hr-day) \qquad\qquad\qquad\qquad (sec-min-hr-day)

RECORD Each occurrence of Pinpoint		CONSEQUATE Consequences following occurrence of behavior					EVALUATE Each occurrence of Pinpoint		
Date	Obs #	Date	Obs #	Approval	Dis-approval	Other	Date	Obs #	

Total = _____   Totals = _____   _____ _____   Total = _____

\# Obs. = _____   \# Obs. = _____

Average = _____   When _____   When_____   Average = _____

Comments _____

(appropriate)

_____ for _____

_____ (time-times)

_____ Then these approvals will follow:

(inappropriate)

Then this disapproval will follow:

Summary:

Record total _____

Evaluate total_____

Record average_____

_____ a. _____

_____ b. _____

_____ c. _____

a. _____

Evaluate avg._____

Increase_____

Decrease _____

General Observation Form

PINPOINT_____ Person(s) observed_____

Observer(s)_____ Location_____

Time of obs. _____ Desire that behavior increase decrease

I (we) will conduct _____ observations per _____ every _____ for _____
                (number)   (min-hr-day)   (day-wk)   (day-wk)
before consequating takes place.

Observation interval _____ Time between obs. _____
                    (sec-min-hr-day)   (sec-min-hr-day)

RECORD — Each occurrence of Pinpoint			CONSEQUATE — Consequences following occurrence of behavior					EVALUATE — Each occurrence of Pinpoint		
Date	Obs #		Date	Obs #	Approval	Dis-approval	Other	Date	Obs #	

Total = _____   Totals = _____   _____ _____   Total = _____
\# Obs. = _____   \# Obs. = _____
Average = _____   When _____   When _____   Average = _____

Comments _____
_____
_____
_____
_____
_____
_____

for _____
   (appropriate)
   (time-times)
Then these approvals will follow:
a. _____
b. _____
c. _____

(inappropriate)
Then this disapproval will follow:
a. _____

Summary:
Record total _____
Evaluate total _____
Record average _____
Evaluate avg. _____
Increase _____
Decrease _____

General Observation Form

PINPOINT _____ Person(s) observed _____

Observer(s) _____ Location _____

Time of obs. _____ Desire that behavior increase decrease

I (we) will conduct _____ observations per _____ every _____ for _____
                     (number)   (min-hr-day)   (day-wk)   (day-wk)
before consequating takes place.

Observation interval _____ Time between obs. _____
                        (sec-min-hr-day)   (sec-min-hr-day)

RECORD Each occurrence of Pinpoint			CONSEQUATE Consequences following occurrence of behavior					EVALUATE Each occurrence of Pinpoint		
Date	Obs #		Date	Obs #	Approval	Dis-approval	Other	Date	Obs #	

Total = _____   Totals = _____ _____ _____   Total = _____
# Obs. = _____   # Obs. = _____
Average = _____ When _____ When _____ Average = _____

Comments _____   (appropriate)   (inappropriate)   Summary:
_____   for _____   Then this   Record total _____
_____   (time-times)   disapproval   Evaluate total_____
_____   Then these approvals   will follow: Record average_____
_____   will follow: a. _____   Evaluate avg._____
_____   a. _____   Increase_____
_____   b. _____   Decrease_____
                        c. _____

General Observation Form

PINPOINT_____ Person(s) observed_____

Observer(s)_____ _____ Location_____

Time of obs. _____ Desire that behavior increase decrease

I (we) will conduct _____ observations per _____ every _____ for _____
    (number)   (min-hr-day)   (day-wk)   (day-wk)

before consequating takes place.

Observation interval _____   Time between obs. _____
                    (sec-min-hr-day)   (sec-min-hr-day)

RECORD Each occurrence of Pinpoint			CONSEQUATE Consequences following occurrence of behavior					EVALUATE Each occurrence of Pinpoint		
Date	Obs #		Date	Obs #	Approval	Dis-approval	Other	Date	Obs #	

Total = _____   Totals = _____   _____ _____   Total = _____
# Obs. = _____   # Obs. = _____
Average = _____   When _____   When _____   Average = _____

Comments _____   (appropriate)   (inappropriate)   Summary:
_____   for _____   Then this   Record total _____
_____   (time-times)   disapproval   Evaluate total_____
_____   Then these approvals   will follow: Record average_____
_____   will follow: a. _____   Evaluate avg._____
_____   a. _____   Increase_____
_____   b. _____   Decrease _____
                      c. _____

210

General Observation Form

PINPOINT_____ Person(s) observed_____

Observer(s)_____ Location_____

Time of obs. _____ Desire that behavior increase decrease

I (we) will conduct _____ observations per_____ every _____ for _____
                      (number)   (min-hr-day)   (day-wk)   (day-wk)
before consequating takes place.

Observation interval _____ Time between obs. _____
                        (sec-min-hr-day)   (sec-min-hr-day)

RECORD Each occurrence of Pinpoint		CONSEQUATE Consequences following occurrence of behavior					EVALUATE Each occurrence of Pinpoint		
Date	Obs #		Date	Obs #	Approval	Dis-approval	Other	Date	Obs #	

Total = _____   Totals = _____   _____ _____   Total = _____
# Obs. = _____   # Obs. = _____
Average = _____   When _____   When_____   Average = _____

Comments _____   (appropriate)   (inappropriate)   Summary:
_____   for _____   Then this   Record total _____
_____   (time-times)   disapproval   Evaluate total_____
_____   Then these approvals will follow: Record average_____
_____   will follow: a. _____   Evaluate avg._____
_____   a. _____   Increase_____
_____   b. _____   Decrease _____
                     c. _____

General Observation Form

PINPOINT_____ Person(s) observed_____

Observer(s)_____ Location_____

Time of obs. _____ Desire that behavior increase decrease

I (we) will conduct _____ observations per _____ every _____ for _____
(number)   (min-hr-day)   (day-wk)   (day-wk)
before consequating takes place.

Observation interval _____ Time between obs. _____
(sec-min-hr-day)   (sec-min-hr-day)

RECORD Each occurrence of Pinpoint			CONSEQUATE Consequences following occurrence of behavior					EVALUATE Each occurrence of Pinpoint		
Date	Obs #		Date	Obs #	Approval	Dis-approval	Other	Date	Obs #	

Total = _____   Totals = _____   _____ _____   Total = _____
# Obs. = _____   # Obs. = _____
Average = _____ When _____ When _____   Average = _____

Comments _____   (appropriate)   (inappropriate)   Summary:
_____   for _____   Then this   Record total _____
_____   (time-times)   disapproval   Evaluate total_____
_____   Then these approvals will follow: Record average_____
_____   will follow: a. _____   Evaluate avg._____
_____   a. _____   Increase_____
_____   b. _____   Decrease _____
                    c. _____

212

General Observation Form

PINPOINT_____   Person(s) observed_____

Observer(s)_____ · Location_____

Time of obs._____   Desire that behavior increase decrease

I (we) will conduct _____ observations per _____ every _____ for _____
              (number)   (min-hr-day)   (day-wk)   (day-wk)
before consequating takes place.

Observation interval _____   Time between obs. _____
              (sec-min-hr-day)   (sec-min-hr-day)

RECORD Each occurrence of Pinpoint		CONSEQUATE Consequences following occurrence of behavior					EVALUATE Each occurrence of Pinpoint		
Date	Obs #		Date	Obs #	Approval	Dis-approval	Other	Date	Obs #

Total = _____   Totals = _____   _____ _____   Total = _____
# Obs. = _____   # Obs. = _____
Average = _____   When _____   When _____   Average = _____

Comments _____   (appropriate)   (inappropriate)   Summary:
_____   for _____   Record total _____
_____   (time-times)   Then this   Evaluate total _____
_____   Then these approvals   disapproval   Record average _____
_____   will follow: will follow: Evaluate avg. _____
_____   a. _____   a. _____   Increase _____
_____   b. _____   Decrease _____
                        c. _____